# Leadership 3.0

# Leadership 3.0

## A MILLENNIAL'S GUIDE TO MAKING YOUR LIFE YOUR OWN

**Jo Singel**

ISBN: 1514108240
ISBN 13: 9781514108246

## FOR ALL OF THEIR CONTRIBUTIONS

My Son Jonathan

My Husband Don

Good Friends and Colleagues

Michael DiSanti

Peter Fournier

Dr. Anika Gakovic

Paul Gallico

Dr. Carol Gorelick

Douglas Grabowski

Patrice Hall

Denise LeLonde

Cecilia Matthews

Stephen McCarthy

Ellen Reilly

Olga Yavorsky

*Leadership is not for the faint of heart*

*or those who are unwilling to risk what they HAVE*

*for a vision of a future they WANT.*

*Leadership is for the WINNER in life.*

*This book is dedicated to the winner IN US ALL.*


*Jo Singel*

# Contents

# Roadmap for Leadership

"To be, or not to be: that is the question: Whether 'tis nobler in the mind to suffer the slings and arrows of outrageous fortune, or to take arms against a sea of troubles ..." (Shakespeare)

And indeed, that IS the question: whether to float with the tide, or to swim for a goal. It is a choice we must all make consciously or unconsciously at one time in our lives. So few people understand this! Think of any decision you've ever made which had a bearing on your future: I may be wrong, but I don't see how it could have been anything but a choice however indirect — between the two things I've mentioned: the floating or the swimming.

But why not float if you have no goal? That is another question. It is unquestionably better to enjoy the floating than to swim in uncertainty. So how does a person find a goal? Not a castle in the stars, but a real and tangible thing. How can a person be sure he's not after the "big rock candy mountain," the enticing sugar-candy goal that has little taste and no substance?

- Hunter Thompson – 1958

# Prologue

*"Be yourself; everyone else is taken." Oscar Wilde*

## THOUGHTS ON LEADERSHIP
**Don Singel**

Have you ever dreamed about being a leader? Have you ever wondered how a leader is created or how great leaders learn how to lead? Are you one of the people who think leaders are born and not made? Do you wish you had been born a leader? Well, if you've asked yourself any of these questions, I have some great news for you. You can live your dream of being a leader. We all can. Why? Because leadership lives within all of us.

Some seventy plus years ago one of the greatest battles in the history of warfare began – D-Day. The Allies landing in Normandy, France became the defining moment of World War II, as forces initiated the attack that would ultimately turn the tide of the war in the Allies favor. This massive undertaking, which had been planned for over a year, was the culmination of strategic thinking by some of the greatest military minds on the planet. And yet, for as many things that went right, there were significant breakdowns and mistakes that jeopardized the entire mission. The eventual success was predicated on not just the thinking and strategy of Generals far from the action, but by ordinary men who, under the pressure of trying not to just survive, but to achieve their mission, exercised that greatest of all individual attributes – Leadership.

Accountants, schoolteachers, firemen, construction workers, farmers and every other imaginable occupation were represented on the beaches of France that fateful day. All of them thrown into a situation they didn't ask for, with situations and circumstances unanticipated and constantly changing. Those same words can be applied to many of our own daily trials. Every day, in numerous ways, we have our own personal battles. Of course, I'm not comparing the horrors of warfare with the daily aggravations that we either suffer through or try to deal with. However, there is one similarity. Under pressures, stress, or irritation or just working to achieve individual, group or organizational goals, some people rise to the occasion, others falter, and others don't even show up. For some, Leadership is born. For others, the seed, planted within us at birth, lacks the nourishment to make it grow and thrive.

When human beings are diagnosed with poor eyesight, their eyes are evaluated and a variety of solutions are provided so that their vision is corrected. Allow this book to become both your empowerment and vision for allowing your leadership to blossom and grow. This book is dedicated to every person who has thought to themselves "I wish I could be a leader". Some yearn for it, some grasp for it, some shy away from it. Leadership lives within us. Possibility lives. Yes, there is a leader within us all.

# The Mission

Educate you and others who want to learn how to communicate value as a leader in life. Enable you to create more choices, opportunities and possibilities to do work that has meaning, is purposeful and has a positive impact.

# How This Book is Organized

The ROADMAP is a framework for lifelong learning. Accelerating, optimizing and enhancing capacity to learn, tools for creating targeted, measureable and impactful goals, creating and executing on a vision for a lifetime of experiences that are meaningful and make significant contributions.

The book is organized around three levels of learning achievement: Basic, Advanced and Mastery.

Each level has a focus:

- **Developing Leadership Mindset**
- **Building Courage Muscle**
- **Becoming a Leader of Leaders**

Content targets three levels for developing awareness:

1. Self
2. Others
3. External Environments where leadership vision and goals can be executed and achieved for impact.

**By the end of the book, if you can identify and execute on three or four areas for a lifetime of learning and achievement, you will leave a legacy of meaningful and positive contribution.**

**WHERE AND HOW DO YOU WANT TO LEAVE YOUR MARK FOR FUTURE GENERATIONS TO BENEFIT?**

## Where To Begin

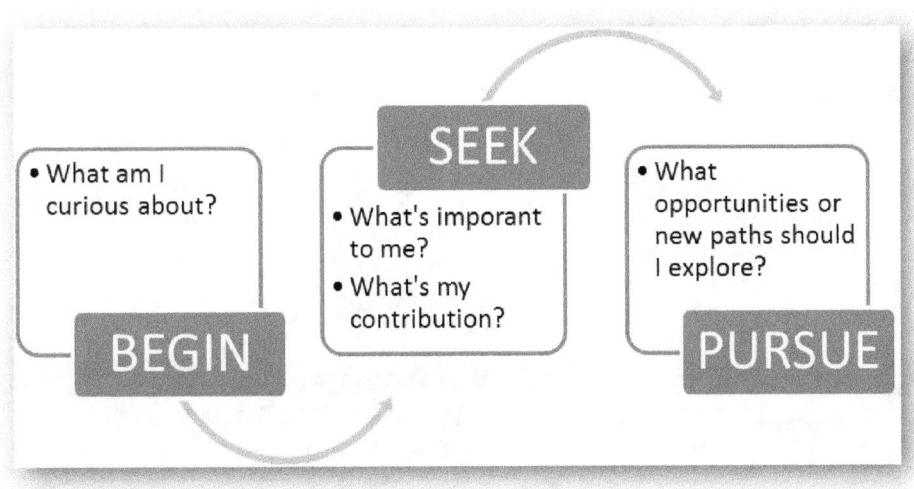

# Being

# Basic:

## Developing Leadership Mind-Set

**Be Curious & Think**

# Turbulence Ahead

magine you are seated in a jumbo jet that has cruised smoothly down the runway. The plane safely achieves lift off and you are gradually and steadily climbing 10,000, 20,000 and ultimately 30,000 feet to achieve your cruising height.

You are finally relaxing and are looking forward to removing your seat belt and standing in the narrow aisle to stretch your legs that have been imprisoned by the cramped space you have been occupying during the flight.

No sooner than you complete the thought, the overhead light blinks and you can hear the gravelly sound of the airplane's intercom system. The pilot clears his throat as he prepares to make an announcement. You expect good news; with a good tail wind, you might arrive at your destination ahead of schedule. Instead, the pilot describes a less desirable scenario. There will be unexpected and severe turbulence caused by a fast moving weather pattern that suddenly appeared on the radar. The jet stream is not behaving according to its predicted path. "Out of the blue" the jet stream took a sharp angled right turn instead of a more even keeled left one. As a result, the pilot will be required to course correct. As a necessary precaution, he requests that you store any belongings that could harm you or other passengers. You moan in discomfort and pull your seat belt to secure it more tightly around your body.

What has happened is that in a matter of minutes the pleasant and uneventful picture you had painted for your journey is quickly vanishing. Your fantasy has been interrupted by the unexpected. "Sorry folks", says the pilot. "Prepare yourself for a choppy ride." The change that has occurred was not predictable and therefore decisions will be made in the moment rather than in a step-by-step and linear manner. The pilot's previous experience, judgment and instincts will all be called into play as the flight proceeds.

The turbulence begins and the plane is tossing like a toy boat caught in rough seas. Instinctively, you know that this is only the beginning. Your heart is palpitating and you can feel the beads of perspiration forming on your upper lip. You don't want to show it, but you are afraid. You notice your fellow passengers are looking around and, as you turn in your seat, someone catches your eye. You smile and, nodding your head, feel somewhat comforted that you are not alone in this situation. Nearly everyone is feeling the same at this point in the journey.

Nonetheless, the plane continues to rock and you have no idea how long the disruptive and uncomfortable turbulence will last.

The only recourse you have is to remain calm and focus on a positive outcome.

# Survival

What has been described in the prior scenario is the type of situation leaders can and do encounter on a daily basis. Whether in work or life, change arrives unannounced. Strong and unexpected turbulence can quickly interrupt ones world. Something changes and decisive and quick action is necessary.

Now and then, not only are external changes disturbing the natural flow of events, but at times our core foundation is challenged as well. The beliefs, perceptions and assumptions that have served us well can prove useless in the face of sudden, unexpected and unforeseen intrusion into the routines of our daily lives.

But wait a moment. In the airplane scenario described, you were the helpless and passive passenger strapped into the chair, feeling out of control and powerless, hoping the pilot is experienced enough to get through the storm safely.

Isn't this a book about leadership? In this story shouldn't you, the aspiring leader, be sitting next to the pilot, learning and observing so you will know how to deal with emergency situations?

That would have been a book about yesterday.

THIS IS A BOOK ABOUT TODAY AND THE FUTURE!

What follows is information and knowledge on how you can create the future you want.

# How Can You Create A Powerful Future?

USE THESE SIX KEY ACTIONS TO DISRUPT YOUR FUTURE AND ACHIEVE IMPACT

- ☐ **BE CURIOUS**

Where would you like to have impact? Make a difference? Create value for yourself and others?

- ☐ **THINK**

How and where to DISRUPT AND INNOVATE what already exists, into a vision of what can be. Disruption is an essential part of change. Without change, there is nothing new.

- ☐ **DISRUPT**

Create a plan. Take action. What worked? What didn't work?

- ☐ **INNOVATE**

Implement the changes. Test your ideas against reality.

- ☐ **CHANGE**

Interrupt the status quo. Help others make the change into a new way of doing things.

- ☐ **IMPACT**

Measure the impact of what you created and implemented. Share the results. Help others learn from what you did to disrupt and innovate a new idea or vision,

It is time to IGNITE your passion for doing something meaningful with your life and FERTILIZING your ideas into your vision for the future.

First, let's examine the current reality. What challenges and opportunities await the creative, disruptive leader?

# Today's World

## THE CURRENT REALITY

In today's world, there is increasing complexity and uncertainty creating an abundance of confusion and doubt concerning ones ability to safely navigate the rough terrain. There will be situations when reflection, careful analysis and research will need to be placed aside. Although risky, taking quick action is the only sensible solution.

As in the scenario involving the pilot and passenger in the story presented, those aspiring to be in leadership in life will need to seize the opportunity to shift from being the passive passenger to the pilot in command. Oftentimes, there is no invitation to such a task.

And that is how it's done, without months and years of preparation, observing and practicing based on the actions, guidance, advice and wisdom of others.

There are very few, if any, "apprenticeship" situations for aspiring leaders. Perhaps there never were those opportunities available to the majority who were expected to accept their lot in life. Instead they were set on a course of following the lead of others, accepting direction, and doing what they were told.

If you choose to set your own course and direction for your future, you will need to side step the meticulous, organized process of growing into a sheltered leadership position reserved for a few and incur the cost and pain of learning and developing your capacity as the leader in your life.

Whether you are a leader of "one" that is yourself, or a leader in your family, community or work situation, the fundamentals rarely change.

# Tomorrow's Future

Time after time in speaking, training and coaching individuals who aspire to be in leadership in life, this writer has found that if there was one single aspect each had in common it was the desire to have an impact, make a contribution, and leave a legacy no matter how great or small.

Rarely does the individual talk about a material legacy but rather an ideal, a history of accomplishment based on a personal vision, a core belief or set of values that dictate they blaze a new trail. In some instances it involves setting out far from home to begin a new life and achieving deeds that were not approachable for their parents or grandparents. Or, in some cases, the individual decides they wanted to create goals on their terms and not those set by others such as the family, social institutions or business organizations.

Frequently they gladly offered time and resources to those who had a similar quest. They were eager to share what they learned and happy to know that others wanted to discover new talents or open up new opportunities for themselves and others.

In terms of achieving their goals, in life and in work, their desire was and is to have an impact on the social environment in which they live and for a future generation.

*What is your "impact" going to be?*

*What is it that you want to achieve that will live beyond your time here and have an impact on your world?*

# Who Do You Admire?

---

Take a look at the people you admire most. Do an internet search. Find out what they do, what groups they belong to, what they share about themselves. Ask yourself what you like about them and what it is you can do RIGHT NOW to begin meeting people like them.

Oftentimes, our circle of friends and communities provide a level of comfort. It's time to reach beyond the comfort zone and tackle new opportunities to learn, be challenged and think outside the box.

BE A GIVER

Where do you want to devote time and energy to something where you are the GIVER rather than the RECEIVER of value?

Brainstorm a list of areas where you want to make a difference.

What would you like to accomplish and how will you measure the result of your effort?

**Be a deliberate creator.**

*Be a student of the world around you.*
*Know it.*
*Formulate a unique opinion and be able to express it in a compelling way.*
*Have passion.*
*Be compassionate*
*Have the courage to stand out on the limb alone.*
*Risk more.*
*Be more than you ever thought possible.*

# Are You Making an Impact?

---

Every living creation on the planet leaves behind some residue of their visit.

Whether that is a footprint in the sand or a human being leaving a legacy for future generations, a work of art, or having helped another.

For better or worse, everyone is having an impact on the society and environment in which they live.

An individual's impact is the sum total of their life's purpose, mission, or work regardless of how great or small. The very fact that they existed leaves, in their absence, an imprint.

This book is about the impact or legacy of your having lived. It's focus is on assisting you in taking stock of who you are, what you are doing, why you are here and what difference or impact your life will have had far beyond the time when you have physically existed.

**The result of your leadership aspiration is your "impact".**

# Change Either Happens to You or You Anticipate it and Get Ahead of it

P lan for it or initiate it. No matter how it happens, the process is the same.

*You are changing jobs...*
*You have recently graduated from high school, college or graduate school...*
*You are frustrated with your current situation and want a change...*
*You want to be an entrepreneur...*
*You want to do work that is more meaningful...*

Most of the time, the urge to make a change or take a different course of action is when we are most open to considering alternatives. Rarely, however, do people take time to think about what got them to their current condition. Oftentimes, without careful consideration of the present and past, the cycle repeats itself and they wind up back where they were.

**Now is the time to BE CURIOUS and THINK!**

Before you become locked into a role or particular responsibility that is difficult to change, consider other possibilities. Depending upon your level of curiosity, determination, stamina, will-power and perseverance, life will feel like a burden to bear, a minefield of problems, or a treasure trove of opportunities.

Most people will take the less stressful path and ask friends or family for their opinions and advice. They hesitate to jump off the well-trodden path without assurances and a firm safety net. Although most safety nets tend to be illusory and temporary, people strive for stability and comfort. Unless you are in a small percentage of the population who are outliers and natural born risk-takers, it's going to take a jolt to take the leap of faith required to change.

Anyone who has had the opportunity to coach or mentor a more junior individual just starting out on their job, career or chosen profession would agree that on more than one occasion they've had to caution the individual about following the advice of another.

Yes, you can seek guidance, ask for feedback, and listen to an experienced individual's stories and lessons learned. However, in the end it is you who are the decider. Not your partner, friend, neighbor, classmate or colleague at work.

Excusing yourself because of your circumstances, environment or pressure from peers does not exempt or prevent you from taking ownership of your circumstances.

Taking responsibility for your choices and decisions is not about morality or judgment of good versus bad. First and foremost, it is a decision, conscious and willful, to be the sole authority over your own self that includes your body, mind, spirit and attitude.

Consider the following dialogue between John and Mary.

Mary:   Why did you make those particular choices or decide on a particular course of action?

John:   I chose to make those decisions based on my own research and what's important to me.

Mary:   Weren't you afraid of making a mistake?

John:   No I wasn't. I'm responsible for the outcome of my actions and attitudes, not anyone or anything else.

Mary:   I heard it didn't turn out so well for you. Don't you feel terrible about it?

John:    I don't feel badly about it. I learned a great deal and now I'm going to use that knowledge to try a new approach.

That is what an individual who is a leader in their life would say and that is how they would respond to another's inquiry into their actions or activities. Decisions were made and paths taken. It couldn't be simpler than that. What it often is – is UNCOMFORTABLE.

There are few if any short cuts on a self-initiated path of growth and development. On some days only disappointment and frustration will be the reward. Doubt will trigger fear and anxiety, eventually leading to confusion. But never must apathy or inertia overwhelm the positive goals. Even when there is uncertainty, taking action is important. This is why self-reflection and a deliberate plan with clear and measurable milestones are key to successful outcomes.

There are individuals who sleep a good part of their life away. Once an individual is enveloped in this state of being it can be very challenging to make the shift to less destructive behaviors.

There are individuals who grope their way through every day and night, wandering aimlessly, spending hours on social media sites. How did they arrive at that point in their life? It isn't difficult. They got there by existing and not living their lives in action or activities that built their sense of self worth, enjoyment of life and strong relationships.

They have little or no energy for any other person than themselves, with few inner reserves or resources to give to their families, communities or friends.
They have disappeared and are invisible to the world around them.

*Are you visible to the world around you?*

# Visibility in the World

IN WHAT WAYS ARE YOU INVISIBLE TO YOUR WORLD?

WHAT WILL YOU NEED TO DO TO CHANGE THAT CONDITION?

# Continously Assess your Current Reality Against your Vision

IT'S IMPORTANT TO BUILD DECISION-MAKING SKILLS

Ask yourself:

*Are you the leader of your life? If not you, then who is?*

Can you live a life where, at every turn, you must ask someone else for the answers to your questions or critical life-changing decisions?

The question "What do you think I should do" should only be asked after you have done your own research and can intelligently share what it is you would like to know.

Asking another human being, "What should I do" is an act of transferring the responsibility of decision making onto their shoulders. It is not a fair question. The person doesn't know or understand your circumstances, financial situation, talents, how you think, and what resources you have in order to provide you with a good answer.

It's challenging to convince people that the journey is best taken with a near empty satchel, generous amounts of curiosity to learn, test and experiment with new ideas.

Think of yourself as a marathon runner. You are competing with your own best self. Looking around to see where everyone else is in the race is a waste of time and energy. It is difficult to maintain focus while worrying about who or what is gaining ground on you.

This guidance is not suggesting a grandiose plan or an attempt to stimulate delusional thinking.

It is about being an individual who is responsible, committed and attuned to the course of action they must take and a realistic assessment of what a good and meaningful life means.

Their measure of success is counted only by themselves and ultimately based upon our own standards.

Society and culture will change with the times. American culture in particular changes more rapidly than others. To name a few, there have been the roaring twenties, beatniks, hippies, yuppies, hip-hop, and many other cultural movements each with their own mode of dress, language and attitudes toward life. Movies, books and art provide insight into each of them revealing the values embraced by multitudes of people during that particular time period.

But what do all of those popular fads and trends mean for individual character, values, beliefs and goals? Should the individual personality, motivations, desires and attitudes be based upon the culture of the time or is it more prudent to set the standards and live by solid principles developed over a lifetime of experience, knowledge and wisdom?

These are a few of the questions you may want to consider as you ponder the bigger challenges of:

1.  Who am I?

2.  What am I passionate about and would commit my entire life toward achieving?

3.  What ROLES are you most likely to play successfully?

Consider:

- Disruptor
- Champion
- Catalyst
- Shaper
- Shifter
- Sherpa
- Influencer
- Connector
- Change Agent
- Initiator
- Implementer
- Problem-Solver
- Change Leader

4. What is my true sense of self worth and how do I maintain a set of values that are important to me and relevant to what I want to achieve?

Some may find that as a result of circumstances and events, their values are not popular. Does this mean they should change? When is change required to avoid being labeled "rigid" and "out of touch with reality"?

*When is adaptation the prudent path of action?*

# What is your Value?

---

Every day there are stories of the rise and fall of celebrities, politicians, heads-of-state, dictators and superstars of the business world.

Reflect for a moment on an individual who rose to great heights in their professions only to end their lives with drugs, alcohol, and suicide. It isn't difficult to easily identify a few of the more well known examples.

"Why, if they had it all, would they ruin their lives and that of their families?"

Maybe we should question the reasons why these superstars are so revered in the first place. Did they possess an individual identity, carved out of their own desires, talents, motivations and needs? Or, were they like the moths drawn toward the flame and burned themselves out for the glory of mass adulation?

## Is that leadership?

In the last century it was.

For the next generation of leaders there is a different kind of thinking going on. Many individuals don't want to be associated with the word "leader". It's interpreted as corrupt, immoral, power hungry, dominating, competitive, aggressive, ruthless and sometimes cruel.

What does the next generation of leader look like? As the title of the book suggests, perhaps we are in the midst of a major shift of what the world wants and needs leadership to be. Millennials and the generation coming after them are beginning to disrupt and innovate what it means to be a leader. They are making news with innovative ways to organize work and compensate employees. Sustainability, social impact and eco-friendly missions are taking the place of pure profit motive. Double and triple bottom line businesses, BCorps, cooperatives and other innovations are just the beginning of a movement toward leadership as shared responsibility for people, planet and profit.

If you are not already there, what can be learned from these "new leaders"? What makes them inspiring and empowering? Are they passionate and committed to different challenges than previous generations of leaders? Do they take different risks and make different sacrifices in service of their vision?

What exactly does it mean to be a leader taking stands and disrupting the status quo in a time when being socially popular and politically correct is the norm?

How do you reconcile the need to be recognized, "liked", and "followed" with the sometimes unpopular task of being opposed to someone's idea, of a different opinion than friends or colleagues, visionary, an "out of the box" thinker?

## Who and what determines the measure of your worth as an individual?

The word leader is not the problem. It's what we, in previous generations wanted, asked for or accepted as the "norm". The next new generation is not aspiring to be the kind of leader that demands, commands and controls others.

Whether called leader, change agent, facilitator, or collaborator, some attributes of ownership and results are timeless.

WHAT LEADERSHIP CAN BE

**Fluid**
**Self-directed**
**Facilitative**

**Collaborative**
**Shared**
**Self-initiated**
**Co-creative**
**Empowered**

Entrepreneurs can partner, co-create, share leadership to set vision, forecast and project, innovate, disrupt, create and get the job done through planning, organizing, prioritizing, educating new talent, growing and evolving.

Perhaps this is who you aspire to be seen as. A role-model, coach, change agent who is focused, has clarity, purpose, sufficient skills, competencies and attributes. Key among these traits are self-determination, self-responsibility and commitment.

Even if you don't aspire to be a leader of others, you will need to be the leader of your own life, work and purpose. In order to accomplish anything significant you will need to:

Establish credibility
Inspire other's confidence and willingness to listen
Empower others to support your goals
Invite others to share knowledge and resources
Build communities of mutual cooperation among all stakeholder groups

Ultimately, who and what we become in our lives is within our control in spite of the circumstances and situations we grow up in, live in and work in.

It can be an enormous struggle to push back history and a society or culture that has told us otherwise.

*What do you believe is within your control in life?*

*What do you believe is not within your control?*

Based on your responses what you have left are your:

- Attitude
- Body language
- Tone of voice
- Speech
- Style of dress
- Mannerisms
- Posture
- Desires

## What you have Left is What is Within your Control.

A critical aspect of being an inspiring and empowering individual is self-awareness.

Begin developing high levels of self-awareness by distinguishing what you think is within your control.

Spending time and energy on tasks, activities and goals that are not currently in your span of influence will cause frustration, stress, confusion and oftentimes, anger at situations and people supporting your idea or point of view.

This behavior will only get you further away from creating something meaningful that you can feel good about.

Testing your idea is essential before investing money and energy into an endeavor that is doomed to fail.

Disrupting and innovating require consideration of the challenges of any kind of change.
If you see yourself as a change agent this is key.

# Develop High Levels of Self-Awareness

B egin with knowledge of SELF.

In your current reality, identify what is within your control and what is not. In areas where you have the most control, you have the opportunity to strongly influence outcomes.

Consider what is important to you and where you want to create value, make a contribution of your talent and time.

In this area, what can you influence that is within your control?

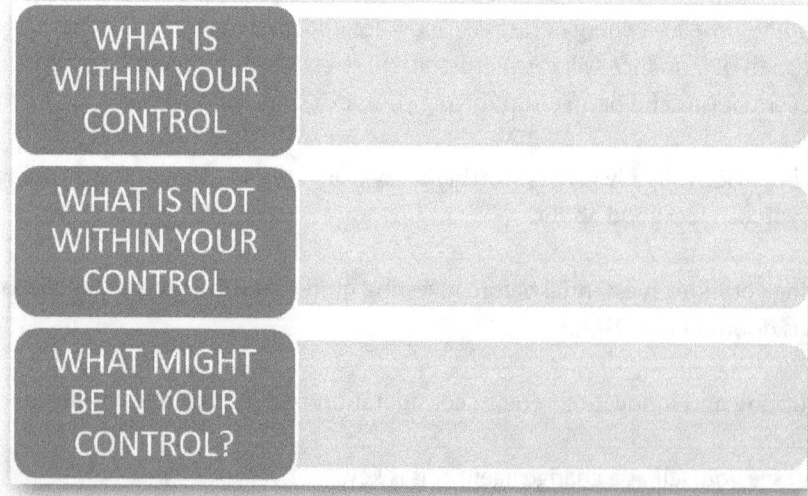

| WHAT IS WITHIN YOUR CONTROL | |
| WHAT IS NOT WITHIN YOUR CONTROL | |
| WHAT MIGHT BE IN YOUR CONTROL? | |

Based on the results of your analysis, are there ways in which you can raise your influence level?

What might you need to learn, do differently or stop doing? Is your behavior influencing your outcome?

Can you scale back your goal and consider smaller steps that can get you closer to where you want to be?

# Get Ready for the Journey

A s with most journeys, there is a greater chance for success when there is preparation and practice.

Important questions:

RIGHT NOW

IN ALL ASPECTS OF MY LIFE

- What's working?
- What isn't working?
- What needs to happen next?

## These Questions Need to be the Top Priority in Any Activity That is Important to the Mission.

Setting goals, planning and determining the best course of action is a wise place to begin.

There is a difference between preparing for an event and embarking on a journey.

*An event is a short-term trip that has a beginning, middle and end.*

*A journey takes place over a longer period of time and is a never-ending process of learning, growing and doing.*

REMEMBER

YOUR WHOLE SELF IS COMING ALONG ON THIS JOURNEY

PHYSICAL, MENTAL, EMOTIONAL, PSYCHOLOGICAL AND SPIRITUAL

# Developing Leadership is a Lifestyle Choice

On the road toward realizing yourself as a leader in life, it is essential that you build a solid foundation in four states of human awareness and being:

- Mental
- Emotional
- Physical
- Spiritual

## Why is this important?

Because as you progress toward developing leadership, the challenges will grow in intensity and you will need to be a stronger person to meet them.

What does being strong mean?

A strong person is someone who can appropriately deal with challenges because they have prepared and made provision for them.

A strong person is someone who has built their willpower and courage by taking on more and more challenging tasks. *Building courage muscles is the same as building physical ones.*

Armed with sufficient and increasing amounts of knowledge and experience including habits, skills, characteristics of personality, values and goals will provide the safety net when the inevitable fall occurs.

Why is it inevitable, you might ask?

When you create a big picture goal or vision, you will fail to achieve what you want many times along the path.

Ask individuals who have achieved great success in their lives. They will share with you that it took many attempts and there were times when they thought they would never see a positive outcome.

## What made the difference for them?

They say it was failing early in the journey. They learned hard lessons. As a result, they felt more confident and focused and continued on the path more determined and wiser than they were before they started.

It takes one step at a time and sometimes taking leaps of faith and rapidly moving in another direction. Always testing, pivoting to a new spot. Taking new actions and experimenting along the way.

Regardless, the temptation to give up the goal in the form of lightening the load with something easier, more comfortable or safer will tempt the achiever.

But if courage, tenacity, perseverance, confidence and stamina have been building inside you, you will have what it takes to continue with your goals.

Practice is essential and all of the small failures you will experience along the way will build your fortitude as you are tested.

*Keep in mind. With all goals and visions there are tests. Sometimes you will need to create a bigger vision, enlarge the scope of what you thought possible and climb another ten thousand feet to get above the clouds that blind you from what you hope to achieve.*

*Remember: This is a book about being a Winner in Life. About Creating and Building a Lifestyle Choice for being a Leader in Life.*

**The difference between success and failure will be how well prepared you are to persevere and keep learning and developing.**

What resources do you have in place before you begin the journey of developing leadership as your LIFESTYLE CHOICE?

# What Are Your Values?

---

Consider this list of VALUES:

- Power
- Commitment
- Passion
- Responsibility
- Accountability
- Perseverance
- Courage
- Tenacity
- Integrity
- Compassion
- Love
- Respect
- Curiosity

Which VALUES hold the most meaning for you?

Which ones do you need to learn more about and build upon?

*The values you choose will sustain you over the course of your journey down the path of developing leadership as a lifestyle choice. They will provide strength and build your stamina, tolerance, patience and ability to take the risks necessary to achieve your goals.*

Your values will act as catalysts, motivators and life support when you need the confidence, tenacity, courage, and perseverance to move forward with your vision.

Choose your values the same way you would choose your friends.

# Who Are You?

Most people will walk around their entire lives without asking themselves this question or never attempt to discover who they are outside of what they were told or what others expect of them.

But as you consider forging a leadership identity, you will find it very difficult to avoid the question.

*How did you get to be who you are today and how did you arrive at your beliefs about life?*

# Being Your Own Best Self

How prepared are you for this journey?

Do the work. Witness the results.

## Begin now.

Identify an individual you know and trust WHO CAN INTERVIEW YOU using the following questions.

1. Who do you admire most and why? What traits, principles, values and actions do those people portray that you respect?

2. How would you describe yourself if asked to limit your answer to three words?

3. What do people count on you for?

4. What would you like people to say about you?

5. What do you like most about yourself?

6. What do you like least about yourself?

7. What would you like to change about yourself?

8. Where, how, and when do you feel the best about yourself?

FINALLY,

*"Am I showing up as an authentic, powerful, self-confident individual who is committed to the work of developing leadership?"*

Rate and score how well you think you did.

(Use a scale of one to five; with five being the highest.)

Ask the Interviewer to rate and score how well they think you did.

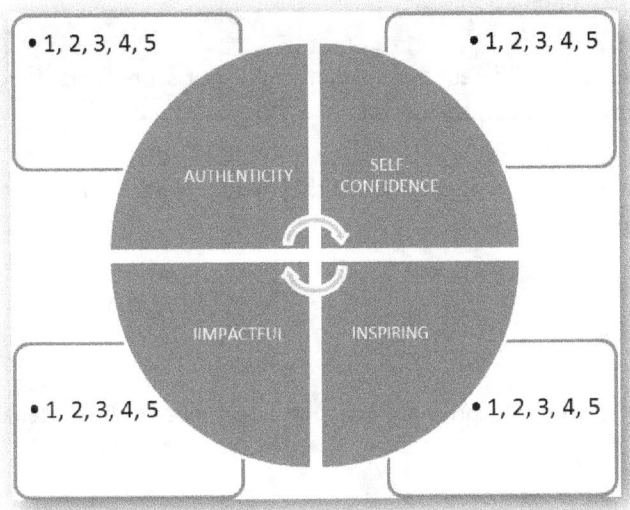

What are the differences between your self-reported scores and those of your Interviewer?

Based on those differences where do you need to improve and in what ways?

## TIP

Unless we ask for specific feedback we seldom know the impact we are having on another individual.

Use the diagram to fill in other attributes such as commitment, responsibility, empowering and others.

Repeat the activity from time to time.

A FEW IDEAS

1.  Use the opportunity to empower your friend or colleague to conduct the same examination

2.  Brainstorm different ways to enhance your scores and share ideas with your friend or colleague

3.  Ask your friend or colleague if they would like to provide feedback and/ or peer-to-peer coaching.

## TIP

Harness the power of communities to support each other's development of leadership.

# Beliefs and Attitudes

USE THE OPPORTUNITY TO ENLIST YOUR PARTNER, GOOD FRIEND OR COLLEAGUE TO DISCUSS THE FOLLOWING QUESTIONS WITH YOU.

- Do you know why you believe certain things to be true?
- Is it because someone taught you what you know or have you carefully examined your responses, attitudes and behaviors?

For example, people engage in relationships which result in unfulfilling situations.

People marry, take on partners, have children and grow into old age feeling angry, dissatisfied, frustrated and confused.

They look around at their life's circumstances and feel regret, sadness and even indignation and resentment toward their loved ones.

Or, there are people who work very hard at their jobs, battling every day to win promotions, move up in their careers only to get to retirement age and wonder where all the years have gone.

There is little or no sense of achievement or accomplishment, only a pension and a monetary nest egg.

They get through the day with repetitive tasks, seeking relief in the occasional family gatherings and sometimes alcohol to ease them into the night.

# Building Courage Muscle

---

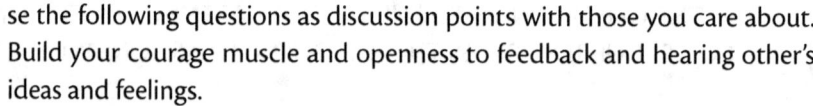U se the following questions as discussion points with those you care about. Build your courage muscle and openness to feedback and hearing other's ideas and feelings.

1. What is your current attitude toward life?

2. Does life feel like a burden to bear, a minefield of problems or an opportunity to achieve what you want?

3. Do you feel caught in the drift of life or are you in charge of your emotions?

4. What circumstances led you to this particular point of view?

5. What people, places and things were involved and over what period of time?

6. Do you use moments, hours, days, months, decades to measure your lifespan and calculate its quality?

# Create a Lifeline

CREATE A LIFELINE OF EVENTS THAT INCLUDE PEOPLE, PLACES AND THINGS
THAT HAVE HAD IMPACT ON YOU

Take a clean, white sheet of unlined paper and proceed to draw a line horizontally
across the middle of the sheet.

This line will represent your "lifeline" that will comprise an overview of the people,
places, events and things in your life – from birth to death.

Mark off increments of between five and ten years, spanning the beginning of your
life to the end of your life.

Now, place significant events such as births, deaths, celebrations, graduations or
other life-altering occasions on the lifeline. Project out into the future of your life.
Where will you be? What events have taken place? What projects have been completed or goals fulfilled? Place each one on the lifeline.

Take a step back and examine what you've determined are the most significant
events that have occurred to you over the course of your life.

Identify important and significant relationships that you have had in your life.
Place them on your lifeline and indicate when you met those particular individuals or groups and when you may have broken off relationships with them.

You are now prepared to analyze the situation. Can you see trends or make connections in between events? Did certain people, situations or things create triggers for future events? Can you see any clear "cause and effect" scenarios?

**Now is the time to reflect upon what you have considered up until this point.**

# Review the Lifeline

Work with a partner to review your lifeline.

Encourage your partner to create one of their own.

Use the following questions to have a powerful conversation that matters.

1. What does your lifeline say about you and your desired state of being?

2. What is missing, if anything?

3. How satisfied are you with your sense of power, presence, self-esteem and personal action plan for obtaining necessary feedback on the principles you are living?

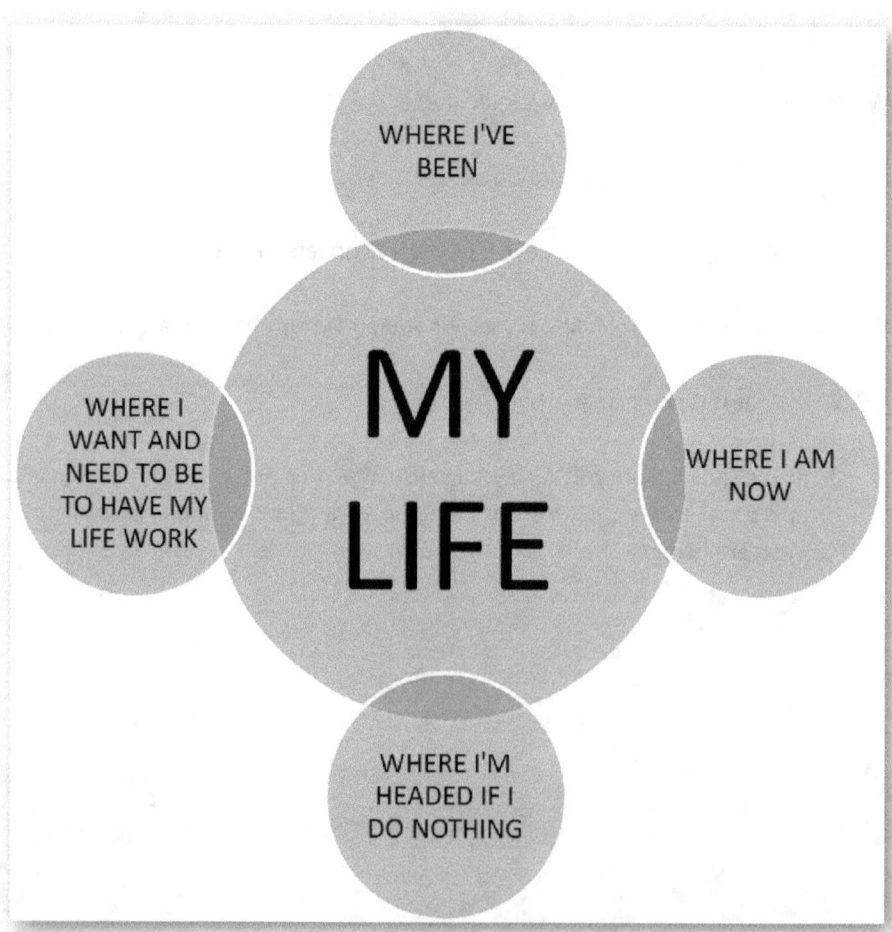

## Assess Current Reality

The lifeline is a perfect tool for assessing the following:

- Where am I now?

- How did I get here?

- Is this where I want to be?

- If not, how and what changes are required as a course of action?

As a result of this activity you will be in a better position to continue a personal inquiry into how you arrived at your current state.

Share your story with a trusted friend or colleague and enlist them in the idea of creating one of their own.

Through conversation, discuss the various high and low points and ways in which you can learn, grow and change as a result of them.

# What Do You Want?

---

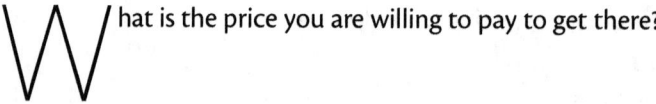

What is the price you are willing to pay to get there?

# Removing the Excess Baggage

magine that the sum total of your entire history is stored in a large closet. Visualize what might be stored there.

Based on what you see or sense is currently stored in the closet, what are you actually using? Conversely, what is being stored that you haven't used in a very long time? What has been tossed to the back of the closet and until now has remained unnoticed, forgotten and gathering dust?

Understand that it takes courage to open up the closets of unexamined beliefs, assumptions and the experiences of our life.  We can never know what we'd find unless we take the first step to look.

For one, there is regret. You may discover things you've forgotten about and wanted to try to hide because you really believe you never should have bought it in the first place. Attempt to set aside some of the mind chatter of accusations and judgments.

What was attractive once can quickly turn into tomorrow's trash. We might think, "What a waste of time, money and energy."  It isn't necessary to identify excuses, reasons and stories for behaving in such a way. It was the best choice you had available to you at the time. Move on and toss out what you no longer need.

It's difficult to discard things that cause feelings of remorse, shame or embarrassment and instead we tell ourselves,

"Well, maybe someday I'll use it. Better keep it here in the closet but push it further to the back."

If the item was expensive you may be tempted to off load it onto someone else. Try not to be tempted to salvage the past. It is of no use or value to you now. You already paid the price for it, no point in paying for it again. It would be futile to attempt to justify past choices and decisions. The mental activity only serves to keep you locked into the past when you took the action that made the most sense. It is in the present that you have an opportunity to make new choices based on a fresh perspective and different experiences.

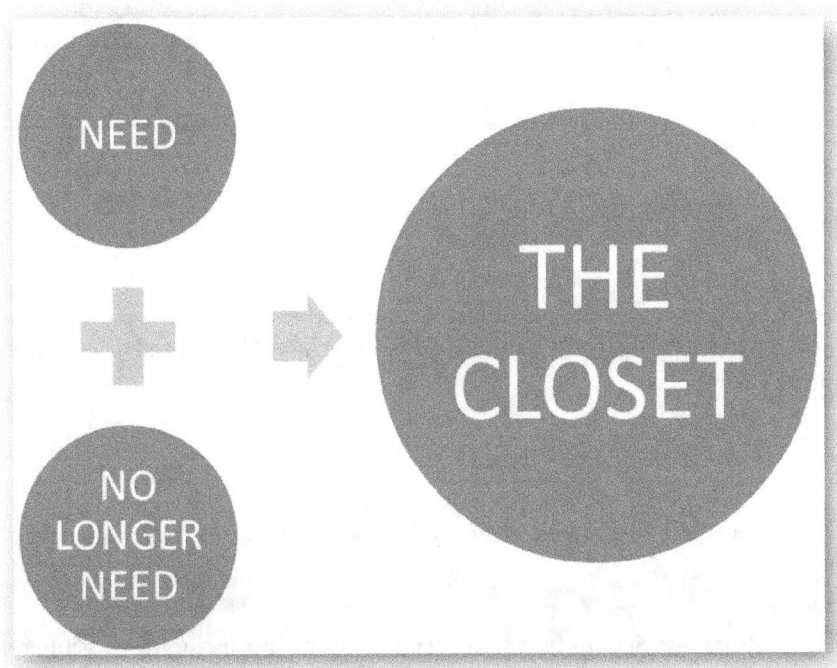

Take time to assess what you need for this part of your journey and what may no longer serve you. There may be people who drain you of energy, environments that are toxic emotionally or psychologically, things that are cluttering your life or outworn habits and ways of behaving that are keeping you back from where you want to be in your life and work.

Take notes as you sort through what is no longer necessary and place certain items in your action plan as reminders

## RELEASING THE PAST

Brainstorm the question:

**What do you need to discard from the past that no longer serves you?**

# In Summary

---

f you have completed the majority of the work in PHASE I you will have achieved the following:

1. Identified areas where you want to have impact

2. Identified Role Models or individuals you admire for what they've achieved

3. Awareness of your best traits, values and talents including possible roles you'd like to play

4. Knowledge of what is within your span of control and what is not

5. Awareness of your current reality, an idea of your vision, your contribution and what you value

6. Identified where you currently have influence and where you could increase your span of influence

7. Identified first steps toward achieving what you want

Identify other areas where you have increased your awareness or thought of ways to strengthen your traits and/or skills.

1.
2.
3.
4.
5.

Now it is time to begin the task of CREATING YOUR LEADERSHIP PORTFOLIO

A few IDEAS:

Build the portfolio with a web application or create a paper-based toolkit using a three-ring binder. It's essential to maintain an organized and structured portfolio that indicates progress, helps to identify gaps in the process and provides positive feedback on progress.

Based on the TOOLS and ACTION ITEMS contained in this book, the portfolio will consist of:

GOALS

AREAS FOR IMPACT

CONTRIBUTION

VISION OF A DESIRED FUTURE

KNOWLEDGE OF CURRENT REALITY

GAPS BETWEN WHERE YOU ARE NOW AND WHERE YOU WANT TO BE

ROLE MODELS

BEST TRAITS & TALENTS

POSSIBLE ROLES

VALUES

AREAS OF INFLUENCE WITHIN YOUR CONTROL

TOOLS

ACTION STEPS

RESOURCES

ACQUISITION OF NEW SKILLS

# Doing

# Advanced:
# Building Courage Muscle

**Be a Disruptor & Innovate**

# What Are Your Habits?

---

eaders must carefully examine the routines and habits acquired over time. It's difficult to be fully conscious all of the time. More than likely, we would hardly accomplish anything since we spend the majority of our time analyzing information, situations and other data that overwhelm every waking moment of our lives.

Habits are those short cuts that help us cope with the minor decisions we must make every day in order to live. Ordering lunch, choosing what to wear in the morning, the time we awaken in the morning and other essential tasks for allowing us to function on a daily basis.

Routines become so habitual we can hardly remember the time when we made other choices.

Not only do we go on automatic pilot with the uninteresting parts of our lives, sacrificing consciousness for the sake of convenience, we also do the same for more significant and important situations whether we realize it or not.

# Assessing Feelings

The following is a list of incomplete sentences designed to spark recognition of what is a routine task and what requires your full attention.

When I need to make a decision I usually...

In order for me to feel good about myself, I...

When confronted I usually...

When I feel uncertain I...

When I feel afraid I...

The results of your answers are important information to digest. If you answer these questions as honestly as you can, they will reveal a great deal about what drives you and what does and does not motivate you to action.

It is important to remember. This is not a book about answers. It is a manual for leaders filled with critical questions that are answered over time and the course of the journey toward full ownership and leadership of one's life.

**This book and the questions it poses are about a lifestyle journey of taking the lead in one's life.**

# Rules

From our earliest lives, our parents or schoolteachers teach us the rules for living a good life. Over time, like our habits, we latch onto prescribed rules that make up the history and stories of our lives. Rules govern our results in very powerful yet subtle ways. When we have a rule about something, no matter what the context of the situation we are facing we reach out, very quickly, for the tool called "our rules".

Rules come in the form of the following:

- How to manage relationships

- Kinds of people to associate with

- Types of careers we engage in

- Our relationship to time

- How we treat leisure

WHY IS THIS IMPORTANT?

RULES act as borders, boxes and boundaries. They block those things that distinguish us from others, provide privacy, individuality, sense of comfort and safety. Sometimes, they become obstacles to what's new, different, challenging and require change. They can also prevent openness, vulnerability and honesty.

Being vulnerable has an upside and a downside. Not enough vulnerability blocks empathy and compassion. It can create a sense of judgment, rigidness and lack of authenticity.

Being vulnerable takes courage. Disrupting the status quo requires risk taking. Vulnerability is being open to taking the necessary risks to step outside the comfort zone to learn, grow, develop and change.

# Having What You Want

---

Reflect on the following questions:

>    What has to happen for you to have what you want?

>    Are your rules helping or hindering you in achieving your goals for success?

>    Which rules propel you forward?

>    Which rules keep you back?

>    Which rules act as guide maps as you create more of what you want in your life?

# How Do You Show Up in Life?

Have you ever noticed that certain people have an energy about them that communicates self-confidence? In emergency situations, they will quickly step out of the crowd to offer help and assistance without being asked or invited.

These individuals exude presence. You can't always define presence but you can recognize or feel it. What you might observe is that a person with presence walks differently than others.

There is an air of self-assuredness about them. You notice them in a crowded room. They communicate clearly, and have an attitude that conveys they can be counted on if necessary or if asked. More often than not, you won't need to request their assistance.

They'll know when to jump into a situation and either take charge or lend a hand in what needs attention. On other occasions, you'll notice the individual when they voice a concern or an opinion. They conduct themselves in such a way that others listen and take note of what they are saying.

## Ask yourself:

Why is that person getting attention when they aren't in charge or sitting at the head of the table? What makes them stand out above the rest? What makes them seem different from the majority of their peers?

Where does this real and non-contrived presence arise? Presence occurs within the individual and can be expressed as:

{
Will-power
Self-control
Self-confidence
Determination
Courage
Being awake, aware and alert
}

Consider the relationship between personal power, attitude toward authority and possessing a powerful presence. How are they related to one another? How does one depend upon another?

# How Effectively Do you Communicate?

n individual who communicates presence in a powerful and confident way clearly projects that they can be relied upon.

## Why?

If you observe the person's behavior carefully you will identify the following activities.

They are:

*Actively engaged in their environment and what is going on around them*

*Focused on what is in front of them and not having silent conversations with themselves*

*Alert to what you are doing and saying while simultaneously remaining tuned into the environment around them*

*Engaged in multi-tasking but treating each task discretely and with great finesse and poise*

*Communicating their willingness and desire to show up in life*

An individual possessing presence is excited, enthusiastic and interested in people and what is taking place around them.

Curiosity, openness, flexibility and eagerness are often used to describe a person with real, trustworthy presence.

An individual with presence will exhibit certain kinds of behaviors and act in particular ways that can be clearly observed.

You will notice them involved in the following:

Reacting in an emergency to help others without being asked or assigned a role

Initiating improvements and following through on the idea

Taking the initiative in a project whether at home, school or work

Calling attention to wrongdoing

Encouraging others to achieve their goals

Speaking passionately about what they believe and value

Energetically getting involved in whatever it is they say they are committed to doing

Offering assistance without a specific invitation

Questioning or challenging the reasons why something is being done in a certain way

# How Self-Confident Are You?

Without a belief in self a leader is like a ship without a rudder and is prone to adopting what is expedient and not necessarily what is authentic and real.

Oftentimes, people become paralyzed by their situations, fears, and inhibitions because they lack the belief that they can actually have an effect on their own circumstances. They feel powerless to take action on their own behalf.

Everyone at one point in time doubts themselves. This is normal and to be expected except when it becomes a persistent state. Doubts raise questions that demand answers.

Leaders should deal with doubt in an honest and thoughtful way, acquiring compassion and empathy for others. This is the hallmark of a leader with authentic presence. Unless and until you go through the experience yourself, you cannot understand what another might be thinking and feeling.

A hallmark for effective leadership is when they are characterized by the following testimonials.

*He/she is such an understanding person.*

*Is a good listener.*

*Has empathy for another's situation.*

*Takes time to comprehend facts.*

*Anticipates what individuals need to learn next.*

*Always takes the time to reward others for a job well done.*

# Identifying Beliefs and Assumptions

Take some time to reflect on your beliefs, assumptions, conditioned responses, past experiences and family legacy that have had an influence on who you are, how you act or be in the world, what you create and what you have accomplished in your life.

## Question:

Who or what has influenced your decisions and has had significant impact on your life?

Recall a time when you felt the urge tugging at you to voice an opinion that you felt would not be popular or others would not approve.

1.   What prevented you from voicing your concern or opinion?

2.   Had you tried before and failed?

3.   Did someone attack you either verbally or physically?

4.   Did you feel ostracized as a result?

## REFLECTION

Write down thoughts and feelings that arise as you recall the scenario that comes to mind.

Now, rewrite the scenario in a way that has you voicing an opinion, taking a stand or sharing your thoughts and feelings.

*How do you feel as a result?*

*What would need to be different for you to take a new action?*

*What blocks or prevents you from moving forward?*

# The Power of Curiosity

---

Original thinking is in short supply and is rarely encouraged whether in school or at work. Be curious about yourself and others. Examine different aspects of a problem or situation. Looking at things differently is a leadership skill that can be developed with time and hard work.

## This is Your Where True Power Lies

Take yourself and others seriously. When challenging assumptions or asking questions, don't accept the standard answers; knock down the institutionalized and clichéd answers. Tear down the walls between you and your own truth.

Attempt to describe what you feel rather than what you think regarding your own answers. Get past what it is you already know and move toward a fresh perspective.

Remember that you are the decider. Your own conscience is the final arbiter of what is right and what is wrong for you and for your world.

# Creating

## Results

# Mastery:

## Becoming A Leader of Leaders

**Being a Game Changer**

# Introduction

The world of work and life today requires a new way of thinking, being and doing. Old models will prevail until traditional ways of looking at things completely shift and change.

This will take time and a new perspective. Until that day arrives, you will need to examine and reflect upon how you will thrive, grow and be successful on your own terms, measures and standards.

There will be numerous situations when the path will not be clear.

People who are in traditional roles of authority, with power over your daily existence, may not have a roadmap to share with you that suits your goals and desires. The new way of being in leadership does not come with a prescribed formula.

The ingredients will consist of your own thought process, field-tested tools and a healthy dose of risk-taking and appetite for challenge.

During the journey you may discover that leadership can be silent, watchful and nearly invisible to others.

The need for leadership can arise spontaneously. Your ability to respond will depend upon your level of preparedness.

There will be no one to tell you exactly what to do in a given situation.

You will have to create the most appropriate path as you make the journey.

What is important to bear in mind is that leaders are not heroes performing su-superhuman feats. They are people who make mistakes, fail, cry, get discouraged and feel afraid. At times, they are indecisive and uncertain of the best course of action. They may whimper when hurt, get angry, feel frustration, throw temper tantrums, complain, and take more than their fair share on occasion.

The difference will be that they will know when to stop and take action.
Are you an individual who wants to disrupt who and what is defined as LEADER?

# What is a Leader?

What is your definition of being a leader?

Does your definition of leadership come from history books? When you were growing up did your parents tell you stories of heroes? Did you gain knowledge of leaders through books or movies? Or, perhaps your favorite cartoon characters or other fictional representations of individuals who fight evil to win the good for civilization were your heroes? Have you accepted as true that anyone in authority is a leader? Is your boss or manager your leader as well?

Understanding who or what means leader or leadership to you is key to coming to grips with this question. Strive to be an original and creative thinker on these questions. There are no right or wrong answers. However, what you think and believe will determine, a great deal of the time, the quality and quantity of your life.

Identifying who and what a leader is doesn't require a particular education or skill-set.

There are numerous business books that will gladly decide for you. However, you will probably not come up with an original thought of your own. Perhaps without realizing it, you will be influenced by another's thinking process. That is why it is important to question, research and look with a careful eye on what it is others want to convince you is the right and true path for you. Yes, you can derive good information regarding the opinions of others. Simply question them. Reflect on and challenge the answers, poking holes and looking for gaps in your understanding.

Ultimately, what you decide will be your own true and real guide.

Crafting an identity that is yours will require patience as you seek to challenge your own thought process and how you arrive at what it is you think you know about life and being a leader.

# Kinds of Leaders

Some people are naturally inclined toward leadership. Early in life, they exhibit recognizable qualities, characteristics, traits, attitudes and aspirations of a leader and are considered as leaders.

Other people learn how to be leaders through the guidance of mentors, role models, teachers, parents, and others who care, are concerned and are good coaches.

Some people quietly take up the leadership challenge without fanfare or great announcements.

Still others learn slowly but with great determination through exposure to others who have a different set of traits, attributes and behaviors.

And ultimately, there are those who rise naturally to a place in their family, society or work where they are trusted, have credibility, are loved and seen as responsible, committed and supportive of the well-being of others.

# Leadership as a Learning Process

Leadership can be experienced as a process, progression and dynamic forward movement from a state of inaction to one of action enabled by commitment, passion, energy and enthusiasm for achieving goals to be satisfied in the near term or future.

It is a challenge to remain committed to a process over a lengthy period of time. We live in a transactional world, moving from event to event, exchanging what we do for what we need to live. Process is uncomfortable for most people because it involves revisiting, revising and learning from what happened before to inform what will or should happen next.

Not every situation in life requires a process to unfold or evolve. However, for long lasting achievement, process is the surest method to deliver the most positive results.

Leadership, as process, is not an event to be achieved. Rather, leadership is a steady, firm, disciplined and multi-faceted commitment with results achieved over time and applied situation by situation.

Perhaps, leadership is an ability, attitude or learned competency that is self-driven and chosen as a way of being in the world.

# What Leadership is Not

As important as it is to understand what leadership is, it's equally critical to identify what it is not.

When you have observed these behaviors in others, how does it make you feel?

Bullying

Aggression

Intimidation

Abuse of power

Need to control others

Cynicism

Pessimistic about people and life

Laziness

Lack of energy or enthusiasm

Excuses of perceived lack of time, money and talent

Lack of concern for others

Being narrow-minded

Stubborn

Willful

Antagonistic

Discuss with a trusted friend your responses to the following questions:

What attributes have you engaged in that have been offensive to others?

What do you need to do in order to address the issues you may have with stubbornness, willfulness, cynicism and other traits that will prevent you from achieving your leadership aspiration?

# The Challenge of Leadership

Have you ever noticed, whether in yourself or in observing others, how easy it is to keep a low profile and wait for someone else to take the lead in an activity or project?

# Empowerment

f you find yourself in a place of inertia, low energy, lacking in passion and commitment to a goal, consider the following:

How many times on a daily basis do you stifle your own opinion about a topic or situation?

How many times do you check in with friends or family, gathering advice and opinions?

How many times do you override your own instincts and follow the judgments of another?

How many times have you wished you had taken more risks for what it is you wanted in life?

How often do you take the time to sit down and consider your next course of action based on your goals?

Based on how you currently feel about sense of self-worth and your responses to the above questions, evaluate whether or not a change in attitude or behavior is necessary at this point in time.

# What is Your Contribution?

Contribution occurs first on an individual level.

Leadership at the level of contribution to family, community and society is challenging.

It is where a person either "shows up" or watches and waits for someone else to do the difficult work of taking a stand or voicing a concern or opinion.

Answer the following questions and examine any insights gained as a result:

1. What does a life of contribution mean to you?

2. What difference do you or can you make that would add value, create meaning and purpose for yourself and others?

3. What difference does your life make to the world?

4. When you die and pass from this life, what legacy will you leave behind?

**If you do nothing differently right now are you satisfied with the result of your life's experience?**

# A Leader Reflects

A Thought

An Idea

A Word

A Language

A Conversation

Energy

Curiosity

Passion

Action

Joy

Happiness

Fulfillment

Contentment

Peace

Perspective

Ideas

Respect

Commitment

Honesty

Integrity

Wisdom

*Our history will dictate our future if we allow it.*

# Preparing for Leadership

A critical success factor in preparing for leadership in life is to reach back to the past and identify outmoded, outdated and irrelevant ideas, concepts, theories, philosophies or attitudes that don't fit the vision of who you want to be now and in the future.

It's important to take a step back and look at what it is you've been carrying around with you throughout your life and experience. What is contained within the mental closet? No matter what your age, background or environment, you've been around long enough to accumulate some useless and even harmful information. Every day the mental closet gets filled with more spam. It can clog your brain and will inhibit or block your awareness so that no new information can filter through to your consciousness.

You are the master of your life. It is time to clear out some of the baggage that has either been taught to you or that you acquired. In order to create a unique and individual identity and leadership presence, you will need to determine who and what you will be in this life.

In PARTS I and II, you worked with material that asked you to identify and reflect on your RULES, HABITS, VALUES and DECISION-MAKING processes. Now, you are ready to claim leadership as your lifestyle choice and not as a burden to bear or duty to fulfill.

What do you stand for as a leader?

What is important to you?

What really matters above all else?

What prices are you willing to pay in order to stand by your values?

Now it is time to begin pulling all of the pieces together.

With a clear mind, your values identified, your learning goal for developing and building your leadership ability is set and in motion. You have a definition or framework for leadership, and you are practicing awareness and presence.
These tools are necessary for continued mental, emotional, spiritual and physical preparation.

## A leader is always in a state of preparedness.

Expect the unexpected but don't get caught up in anxiety, fear, mental paralysis or hesitation. Continue to move forward and stay in action.

Circumstances or the drift of life will always impact us. How we deal with those unavoidable situations can and will make a difference in our lives and those of others.

## Defining Leadership for Yourself

Now that the path has been cleared and the ground prepared, the work of forging a leadership identity is increasing in intensity and urgency. Don't waste time looking back.

Let's move forward and create the future.

# Defining Leadership Identity

G et your notebook and, after careful reflection upon the following questions, write full statements that resonate with your concept of leadership for you and your life.

How do you define leadership for yourself?

What new action can you take that best exemplifies or illustrates your concept of leadership?

Who can assist you in developing your leadership presence and awareness?

Consider a recent event – local, community or the world – that disturbed or upset you.

1. How did you feel about it?

2. Did it make you feel helpless or empowered to do something about it?

3. Is the action you wanted to take within or outside of your sphere of influence?

4. If so, were there a few actions you considered?

5. If not, why not? What can you learn from what occurred and how you felt about the event or experience?

6. If you were a person of influence what might you have done?

7. What can you do to increase your influence?

# Leadership Check-List

AREAS FOR DEVELOPMENT, LEARNING OR IMPROVEMENT

- ☐ Make effective and better decisions

- ☐ Solve problems creatively

- ☐ Take risks and act assertively

- ☐ Set goals and stick with them

- ☐ Prioritize goals and "don't sweat the small stuff"

- ☐ Focus on what's important to the mission

- ☐ Develop and execute on a plan of action

- ☐ Resolve conflicts with compassion, understanding and integrity

- ☐ Build strong relationships with people who embody similar values and goals

- ☐ Listen effectively and be open to different points of view and perspectives

- ☐ Manage time and energy appropriately

Based on the above tool where can you be more effective? Ask anyone who considers themselves a leader what they consistently do and they will tell you that on a daily basis they strive to be more effective.

List them:

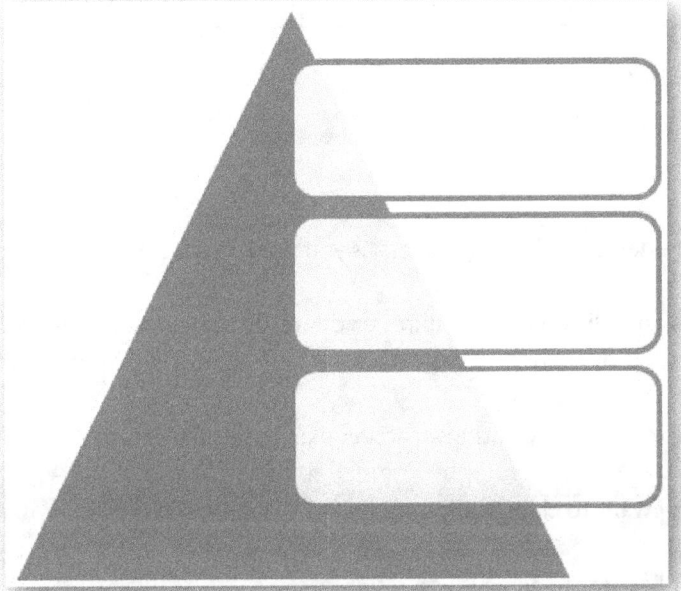

Actions I will take to develop those characteristics are:

Resources I will need are:

My next steps are:

# Developing Goals

---

Consider the following process as you work toward achieving your goals.

As an individual who aspires or desires to strengthen their leadership development, what changes may be necessary as you proceed on the journey?

Take time to consider creating an action plan based on the following:

What I want to change about myself is:

What I expect to achieve as a result is:

Resources I'll need are:

Resources I already have available to me are:

How I'll fill the gap between what I have and what I need are:

My timeframe for change is:

Milestones to be reached are:

Five reasons I need the change are:

Evidence of the change will be new attitudes, skills and behaviors

- The prices I am willing to pay to have the change are:

- My commitment to the change is (on a scale of one to five; five being the highest level of commitment)

# Leadership and Responsibility

Responsibility has always been an important word associated with leadership. It has acquired numerous interpretations and meanings over the years. It's important for you, as a leader, to understand for yourself what responsibility means to you. Does it mean self-sacrifice? Or are you inclined to think of it as a duty or obligation? Whatever your interpretation, your perspective will shift depending upon the lens you are using.

# Being A Leader

Consider how an effective and successful leader in the new world of work would interpret responsibility.

Observe someone you admire who, in your estimation, is taking responsibility for a problem or situation.

- What would they be saying or doing that conveys how they feel about being a responsible leader?

- When you observe or work with an individual who you consider responsible, how does it make you feel?

- What reactions or emotions do you have as a result of being in this individual's presence?

- When was the last time you felt a sense of responsibility? Perhaps you always feel responsible and it comes naturally to you.

- Or, you may never have considered exactly what it means to you and how the very act of responsibility itself is a tool of leaders.

- Consider the consequences of not taking responsibility. How does that make you feel?

- When would you refuse responsibility?

- What if someone were to ask you to do something you thought was unethical or made you feel uncomfortable?

- What would you do then and how would you handle the situation?

- How do your leadership values, principles, goals and activities incorporate the answers to some of these questions?

- In your estimation, what is your definition of a leader who acts with responsibility?

As a leader, I will act responsibly by:
  1.
  2.
  3.

# Leadership Values

As a leader, you will need to gain clarity on your value system. Once you have identified which of your beliefs are self-generated versus imposed by others you may find a gaping hole in what you think you know about yourself. This is to be expected and not cause for alarm. As has already been mentioned, you must be the decider and the chooser.

What values ring true for you as an individual leader? No one will be able to assist you in answering this question. You are totally alone on this part of your journey.

My Leadership Values are:

1.
2.
3.


How I live these values will require me to be:

1.
2.
3.

# Leadership Voice

eadership voice is an inner communication. It is a self-empowering stand the leader takes for their life. The stand may not be articulated but it is assumed and will silently assert itself in all actions. More often than not, it is an inner voice guiding the leader throughout their life.

As an aspiring leader hones his or her values and begins to put them into action, the world begins to respond with feedback. Situations continually arise and you may begin to feel you are always being tested regarding these values. Sometimes people ask if values can change. I believe some values are core to an individual's character and some have more to do with their personality.

A leader's core values are the unspoken strength that people feel as they experience the leader. What and how the leader communicates is felt verbally and nonverbally, as presence, energy and some would say charisma. It is not to imply that charisma or chemistry is a critical or necessary component of leadership. Some people are naturally charismatic and some are not. Charisma is not leadership.

Leadership voice, although more elusive than charisma and difficult to define, is a characteristic of an effective leader. Without it, there is little or no projected personal power.

Examples of Leadership Voice:

*I am the leader of my own life.*

*I value all life.*

*I know and am true to myself.*

*I have deep trust and faith in who I am and all that I can be as a result.*

*I do not walk alone.*

*I am supported in achieving my rightful place in life.*

*I am loved and have love of life.*

# Leadership Vision

The next task in forging the leadership identity is creating a well-defined and clear vision for personal leadership.

What does vision mean in a real time world? Why is this so important?

Vision arises out of intention and is fueled by the satisfaction of achieving what is desired. Knowing that not only do you have the freedom to create but also the opportunity to realize your goal is an exhilarating experience.

Knowing what you desire and having a picture of what it would look like if you were to achieve it is a powerful motivator.

Everyone arrives at their personal vision in their own way.

Some formalize the process by creating a physical piece of evidence of their vision. They create collages, journals, paint pictures, write it in a declaration or statement, purchase a small icon representing their vision or have a strong mental image that they recall from time to time to spur them on when they need a jolt of energy.

Oftentimes, a leader's personal vision is very simple as in, "I want to be happy".

Use these questions to spark ideas:

What is your vision for being a person possessing leadership talent and ability?

What is your vision for the work you want to accomplish in life?

What is your vision for the kind of contribution you want to make as a leader?

First, there is a personal leadership vision. At another level, vision should be created for what the leader stands for, works to achieve or is inspired and motivated by on a daily basis.

MY VISION FOR LEADERSHIP IN LIFE, WORK, THE COMMUNITY AND OR THE WORLD IS:

# Leadership Gaps

As in all goal-setting and planning processes, it's important to identify obstacles, circumstances and challenges that could prevent the implementation of your plans.

WHAT CAN STAND IN THE WAY

What could get in the way of you achieving your vision?

What gaps in learning, knowledge or other resources do you have that could slow down your progress?

What could accelerate achieving your goals?

How can you incorporate the information and knowledge you've learned in reflecting upon your leadership vision into a new plan of action?

I will achieve my vision by:

I will close the gaps between my vision and my current reality by:

I can do more of these things in order to increase my ability to achieve my goals by:

Now that you have identified some gaps, consider new action steps. Vision is an iterative process requiring assessing vision against current reality and course correcting when necessary. There will always be challenges brought on by external forces, circumstances and the "unknown unknowns".

This is why the book reinforces the concept that being an effective leader is a continuous process of LEARNING, CHANGING, GROWING AND DEVELOPING.

This is how a leader remains RELEVANT and a VALUABLE contributor in life, work, family, community and the world.

# Powerful Questions

What would the world be like if many people - regardless of their position, status or economic condition - were to think of themselves as a leader?

How can you assist others to experience leadership as a lifestyle choice?

Remember, the job of a leader is not to create followers but to help create more leaders.

*Learning is essential to growing and changing.*

*A leader's task is to help others learn.*

*A leader always deals with change.*

*Leadership is a state of mind.*

# In Summary

At this point, you have created a vision for your own personal leadership. You have identified obstacles to achieving your desires. You have examined assumptions, beliefs and attitudes that might derail your progress. You've cleared out the closets of past experiences and your history to make room for the future.

Now, as an aspiring leader, you will take these goals, attitudes and desires out into the world and create your own vision of leadership.

Who are you and what is your unique contribution to an endeavor where you aspire to be in leadership? What is the value you bring to who and what you serve?

What you can count on:

- ✓ Being in leadership will place you in situations where all of your thinking will be put to the test.

- ✓ Visions are rarely fulfilled as the complete result of our own actions and activities.

- ✓ Leadership invariably requires that we align, influence, persuade, or sell our ideas and enroll the commitment of others to a common goal.

- ✓ The type of leadership we have been espousing is one in which everyone walks away a better person for having participated in the fulfillment of the goal, idea and mission.

✓ A leader interacts and impacts others throughout the process of realizing the vision and goals.

Your value proposition for any given situation, challenge, opportunity or goal will guide your decisions, communicate your value and act as your conscience as you determine what it is you should and shouldn't do as a leader.

There are certain conditions that nearly always arise during the journey. Not everyone will agree with the leader's vision and gaining commitment is not without its obstacles and challenges.

Leadership is always involved in change of any kind. Whether that is the implementation of a project, an activity or an event, what is required is some level of change and learning in order to achieve the goal. Otherwise, you would be back where you began, going full circle toward having what you already had versus creating something new and different from what was before.

Stepping into the stream, influencing the flow, the direction or the rate of speed is a task that requires skill, planning, strategy and action.

As a leader, you will be accelerating the rate of change creation by understanding the change process, how and why people change or resist the new, and tools for reducing the risk of failure while enhancing the opportunity for success.

To improve chances for success, what follows is a TOOLKIT FOR LEADERS. It will provide further opportunities to enhance, build, develop and strengthen leadership skills, attributes and competencies.

# Toolkit for Leaders

# Contents

# About Learning

ndividuals learn best when they have the tools they need to grow, change, and develop in order to contribute value and have an impact.

Learning begins with the learner's questions and involves identifying goals and achieving results that are quantifiable and impactful.

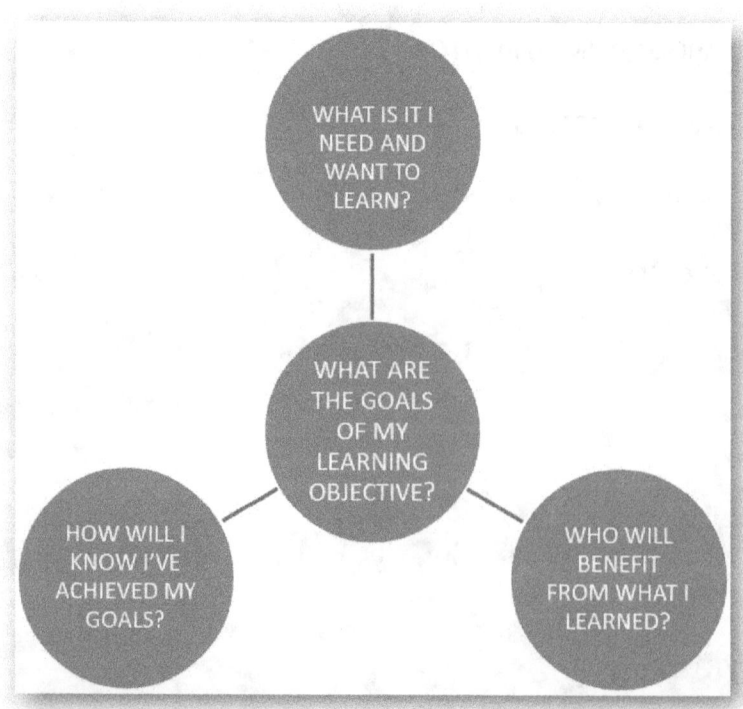

# Learning and Change Coexist

Without learning, there can be no change. Learning itself is a skill. It is seldom taught. Further still, many highly educated people don't know how to teach people how to learn.

By the very nature of being a leader, you will be required to adapt, change and, at times, motivate others to do the same. Adapting, growing and changing will never occur unless an individual or group learns. An active and focused process needs to be undertaken in order to advance beyond the current state of knowledge and experience.

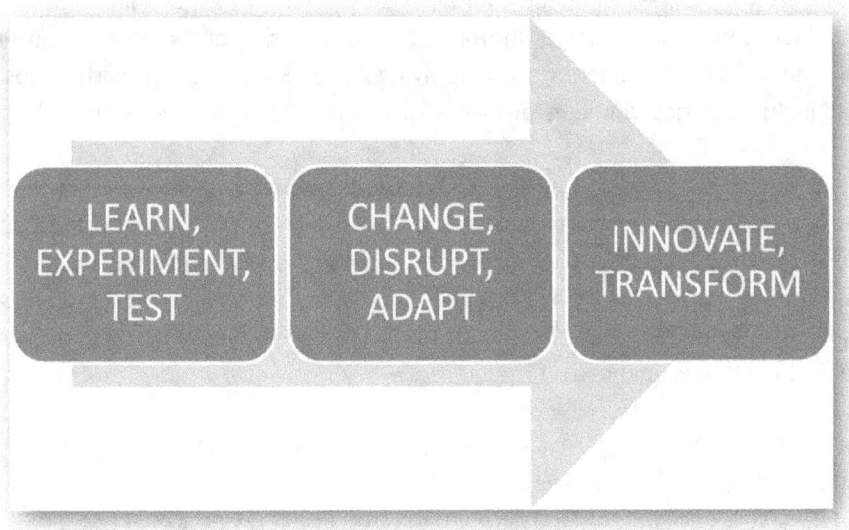

This is an important concept to grasp.

The goal of learning is to acquire new knowledge and experience so as to adapt, disrupt, innovate and transform.

For example, we learn and change in order to do something in an improved way, or in a way that has never been done before. As a result we learn new skills, solve problems differently and stimulate new thinking.

Without the capacity to learn there is little or no change except for what happens as a matter of circumstance or the consequence of an external event. Without learning there is little chance of creating new opportunities or being able to take advantage of them when they occur.

Learning is a proactive state.
Through learning we create.

Oftentimes people are unaware of how they learn in spite of years spent in traditional academic environments. Unfortunately, many children have grown to fear the learning process. Frequently, and throughout an individual's life, learning is conducted in atmospheres of intimidation, competition and demand. Learning routine tasks is very different from applying a process that begins with curiosity and includes critical thinking, problem-solving, risk-taking and decision-making.

Being uncomfortable is a part of learning. Some people experience confusion and anxiety which causes them to avoid learning new things. Being an inspiring leader means we need to understand how some people may feel and their reaction to any kind of change. They may think they are performing well enough and are satisfied with how things are. They have no interest in risking what they know for something that is unknown.

HOW DID YOU FEEL WHEN YOU WERE WORKING ON THE LEARNING ACTIVITIES IN PART I AND PART II OF THIS BOOK?
WERE YOU COMFORTABLE? UNCOMFORTABLE? AT TIMES, CONFUSED?
RELUCTANT TO TRY A NEW BEHAVIOR OR EXECUTE A NEW SKILL?

The inspiration, encouragement, support and vision of another individual can make the difference between successful learning and lack of achievement.

If fear is an obstacle to learning, creating a compelling motivation to change is critical. There is a profound difference between learning in a safe, comfortable, supportive environment where individual differences and styles are respected than in a cold, sterile and uncaring atmosphere.

As we grow into full maturity, the human being becomes more sensitive to failure and mistakes. Humiliation does not increase the ability to learn but only suppresses it. This is why it is important for an individual who aspires to be in leadership to understand how adults learn and the optimal ways in which to conduct an experience that will allow individuals to grow, adapt and change.

The following is a true account of the experience of an adult learner.

# A Learner's Story

---

magine that you have decided, after many years of procrastination, to learn the language of your ethnicity. You want to get closer to your roots and converse in the language of your ancestors. You research the available opportunities and decide to attend a language school. Eager, hesitant, curious and excited to having taken the courageous step of putting yourself into an uncomfortable and unfamiliar situation, you take the plunge. The first day of school arrives. New pens, pads and notebooks fill your carryall bag. The other students are as eager as you are. Everyone is introduced and you wait for the teacher to arrive.

Finally, the door in the front of the room opens and in comes a woman with disheveled hair, obviously pregnant with child and a tired and worn-out expression on her face. It's obvious the woman would much rather be anywhere else but this classroom.

The Teacher plops her book bags on the desk and without much introduction proceeds to let the class know this will be a very difficult term. There will be several hours of homework every night. The class will only speak in the language they will be learning and the Teacher will only converse in the foreign tongue. It appeared from the very heavily accented English any language was going to be a challenge.

Your heart starts racing and you can't understand why that would be the case. You are an adult, not a child held hostage in this classroom. You can leave any time you wish. There isn't any parent asking you about your day at school, wanting to know what your test score was or what homework you needed to complete for the night.

Yet you feel anxious and afraid. The fear is escalating and you feel trapped and alone. What is going to happen here? The class begins and quickly you discover that you will not be able to keep up the pace. Other students have at least some experience with foreign languages. And something you had not anticipated is that the students are very competitive. Getting the correct answer is very important to them.

A week passes and you have now spent four hours each night preparing the homework for the following day's class. As you sit in your chair waiting to be called upon, your hands perspire, your mouth becomes dry and you dread hearing the sound of your own voice. You can't read what is in front of you. You can't comprehend the Teacher's instructions and worst of all, she corrects you and demands that you pronounce the words correctly. There is no respite and the pace is relentless.

Finally, in humiliation, you begin to complain to your classmates. Some drop out in frustration and others sit proudly as they display their fluency. To add further to your insulted pride, you are the only individual in the class who is related to the language being learned. You and the Teacher share a common bond and she is relentless. "Mercy" is not a word in the woman's vocabulary.

You decide you have had enough. You are having nightmares of school years past when you struggled to grasp a math or science concept and stuttered embarrassed answers to the Teachers as classmates giggled.

School days are over for you now and you vow to never try that experience again.

But the story need not end on a negative note. There is an opportunity to prevent humiliating experiences from occurring when in a learning environment.

To provide context for a valuable lesson learned based on this story, consider the following ideas and concepts regarding how people learn best.

# Learning How to Learn

How many times a day does this happen where Teacher and Student, Manager and Employee are in a struggle to teach or learn something new? Most of the time it isn't so easy to quit. Fear, intimidation, humiliation, shame and embarrassment ruin many lives and stifle creativity and the potential contribution of an individual. Children quit school, fail to graduate and refuse to undergo the degrading experience of not being able to learn.

If you see your role as inspiring others to be in leadership in their work and lives, learning how to learn and helping others learn is an important step toward creating an individual identity and a leadership presence that is unique and powerful.

When a person who is in leadership in life can help others learn, the contribution to another's life is enormous. Every adult who has forgotten what it is like to be a child, who stumbled, struggled for one reason or another with a homework or classroom assignment should take a class in a subject that would be a challenge. Experience is the best teacher. And having the experience freshly in mind will close the case on why it is vitally important to understand what learning involves.

You don't need a college degree to learn simple, basic fundamentals about learning that can and will make an enormous difference in what individuals will be able to achieve as a result.

What else do you need to know about learning?

The best place to begin is with ourselves.

The aspiring leader must identify how they learn best. This can be effectively accomplished through practice and trial and error. First, the leader must understand what learning is and means, how people learn and what obstacles stand in the way of learning.

CREATING A SAFE AND SUPPORTIVE ENVIRONMENT FOR LEARNING IS KEY TO HELPING SOMEONE LEARN. THIS IS IMPORTANT TO REMEMBER WHEN INITIATING OR EMBARKING UPON A DISRUPTIVE, INNOVATIVE CHANGE THAT WILL REQUIRE SIGNIFICANT AMOUNTS OF BEHAVIOR AND ADDITUDINAL MODIFICATION.

- BUILDING AWARENESS FOR THE NEED TO CHANGE
- COMMUNICATING NEW INFORMATION AND KNOWLEDGE ACCORDING TO THE LEARNER'S CAPACITY
- EDUCATING FOR THE ADOPTION OF THE CHANGE
- MEASURING SUCCESSFUL ADOPTION
- PROVIDING FOR CONTINUOUS LEARNING AND INNOVATING FOR IMPROVEMENT

# Principles of Learning

- ✓ Involves unfreezing from one state of knowing something to another

- ✓ Always involves refreezing into a different state from the current state

- ✓ Has an objective otherwise we wouldn't know what to expect as a result of our efforts

- ✓ If successful will always cause a shift in perception, perspective or behavior

# Ways We Learn

People learn by:

Experience - by doing; activities

Reflection - self-awareness

Observation - paying attention and listening

Clarification – understanding

Feedback from others

Reading and applying the new learning

Role-Models

Mentors and Coaches

Powerful questions that challenge current perceptions

## Reflect upon how you learn best.

WHICH ITEMS ON THE ABOVE LIST REFLECT HOW YOU LEARN?

What do you need to enhance your learning skills?

What prevents you from learning?

What is the optimum environment for you to learn?

Do you need to watch, listen and then experience the new skill or behavior yourself?

Do you need someone to coach you through the new activity while providing continuous feedback?

Oftentimes people confuse learning with training and consider both words to be interchangeable. They are not.

Learning is an active process of raising a question or hypothesis, "what do I want to know about a topic"; testing various responses through research or trial and error; taking action on the information and finally reflecting upon the outcome.

Reflection involves self-discovery and occurs in many ways. People learn differently and at their own pace based upon motivation, desire and need.

Helpful questions will guide the learner toward their own conclusions:

- ✓ Did I learn from the situation?

- ✓ What was gained as a result?

- ✓ What worked well or didn't work so well?

- ✓ How do I apply what I learned to similar situations or to gain further knowledge of my topic or subject?

If and when learning occurs, there will be a change in behavior, attitude and sometimes, beliefs.

# Strategies For Successful Learning

Leaders should apply thoughtful consideration to the following questions whether applicable to self or others:

1.  What will the participants see, hear and feel during the experience?

2.  Are there attractive, informative, well-presented visuals that reflect what is to be learned in the session?

    *   Motivational proverbs and inspiring visuals help

3.  What is the physical environment communicating?

    *   If it's dull, boring, dirty, and uncomfortable, a message is communicated that people won't be respected and the learning won't be taken seriously. People may not understand this on a conscious level but they will experience it on a subliminal one.

    *   Does the physical space appear as though it had been prepared for the people in attendance?

4.  Are there adequate resources available such as flipchart paper, a black or white board with proper marking pens and erasers?

5.  Are there articles, websites, and check lists available after the learning experience to reinforce what was presented?

    *   Are they attractive, free of typos and in sufficient quantity?

6. How is the seating arrangement presented?

   - For highly interactive sessions, a circle is best.
   - In more self-reflective work, chairs facing forward are effective.

7. Is there proper ventilation, not too hot or too cold?

8. Does the facilitator's appearance reflect and convey professionalism in such a way as to create credibility and respect?

9. What materials have the participants received prior to the session to prepare them for the experience?

10. How will successful learning be measured? By whose standards?

11. Do the participants have follow-up activities?

    - Learning is a process that needs to be applied and is acquired over time. It doesn't happen overnight. People will not suddenly walk away changed no matter what the threat is or how persuasive the argument.

12. Did the participants create a personal goal for the learning and a way to measure progress?

13. What resources, in the form of coaches or mentors, will assist the individual's learning process?

14. Is there a follow-up meeting scheduled where individual stories can be shared, lessons learned are identified and encouragement freely given?

Authentic, caring and compassionate leaders understand and take the time to prepare an environment that is psychologically safe, physically comfortable and attractive. They provide appropriate resources and are available for guidance and support.

# Knowledge is Different from Information

Oftentimes, people mistake information they gain as knowledge learned. Information and knowledge are not the same. Information is easy to acquire and changes rapidly.

Information is cheap and comes fast. Knowledge is expensive and is acquired more slowly and over time. Information has a short shelf life. Knowledge gained from experience lasts longer and is more difficult to unlearn. That is why learning comes with a price tag. You need to let go of what you know and allow for the new awareness to take hold in your experience. Until then, you may feel uncomfortable, confused, and desperate for answers. The longer you can stay open and questioning the better. A tolerance for ambiguity is essential. You will "live in the grey" while acquiring new knowledge.

It takes discipline and focus to learn.

Good learning practices:

1.  Discover as much as possible about your learning goal.

    •   Identify what it is you want and need to learn.

    •   Be specific and create ways to measure your progress.

2.  Identify opportunities for learning how to achieve the goal.

3.  Determine through trial and error what it is you need and want to learn.

4. Ask what resources others have used to achieve their learning goals.

   • Specifically, where did they go to learn what they wanted and who are the best teachers? What books, websites and/or other written materials were useful?

5. Identify challenges to achieving the learning goal.

   • What might hinder you from learning your topic? Is there some skill you would need?
   • How can you go about acquiring it?
   • Can you barter with someone who is expert on the topic and exchange your knowledge for theirs?

6. Create a situation where you can test your newly acquired skill.

   • Is there a situation that would provide an opportunity for building skills or gaining knowledge and expertise?

7. Find trusted colleagues who will provide you with feedback and additional resources.

   • Test and measure your progress against the feedback you receive from others who are aware of your goals when you began your learning journey.

8. Seek a coach you know and respect and who knows and respects you. This can be the most valuable source of feedback.

   • Identify ways to repay your coach for the time they have taken to provide you with valuable input regarding your learning goals. Perhaps they require an occasional technology fix or other situation where your skills can help them to achieve their goals.

9.  Conduct an After Learning Review.

    - What was it that you started out to achieve?

    - Where are you now regarding the goal?

    - What is still missing?

    - What will you do to address the gaps?

10. Develop a plan for continuing the learning process. Identify who, what, where, when and how you will continue to work on your learning goals.

# Empowering Learning When Initiating Change

Rarely will anyone embrace the unknown in favor of the known even when it is in their best interests to do so. And this is understandable. Our habits, attitudes, beliefs, conventions, rules and traditions define who we are – they are our collective and individual identity – hard earned, comforting, and nearly unchangeable.

As we go through life, we become increasingly accustomed to a daily process of adjusting and reacting to our internal and external environments and events all in an effort to maintain our equilibrium. Otherwise we feel lost, afraid, abandoned and insecure. These are feelings and emotions that we will do anything to avoid. They tie us up in knots of uncertainty and confusion and cause us to become paralyzed and unable to move in any direction.

Consequently, when we are asked to change, our very identity is being called into question. We may feel that we are being judged or wrong and that everything we've ever known, counted on, or been valued for will be lost. Then who will we be, what will we do, how will we survive in a world that is so vast and so confusing? Who we are is intricately tied up in what we do and have. Change will alter all that is known, tried and tested through hard-earned life experience.

Why would there be a need to change what has worked so well up until now?

Your task as a leader is to present a vision that is powerful, compelling, understanding, clear and that will outlive the benefits, risks and rewards of changing or not changing.

The case for change must be seriously examined and reflected upon for flaws, personal biases, and perceived realities.

Change for the sake of change is not a reason to change. But change is constant and you, as a leader, will need to demonstrate that being ahead of the change is far less threatening than being at the effect of the change that is imposed from someplace outside of oneself.

# Leadership Task: Sharing Your Story

The leader's personal life story is a powerful tool that can be used to engage others in committing to a vision.

The elements are your vision, the mission, goals and a value proposition.

Consider carefully what it is you share about yourself and how you frame your life's experiences, goals and desires to communicate what it is you want to achieve.

Reflect upon these questions:

What is the story of my life?

What were the challenges I faced early in my childhood?

- How did I overcome them?

- Who helped me?

- What hindered me and why?

- What did I learn from these experiences?

- What do I want to start doing, stop doing, and continue doing that will enable me to approach life fully confident that I have the capacity, the intelligence and the wherewithal to engage life as fully as possible?

## Write a script that tells your story.

Two or three pages of typed material are sufficient.

Put a title on the top of the sheet, sign and date the document.

You are now on your way to creating your biography, which is different from your resume.

Your biography is your story, in your words, which communicates your journey.

It could include your background and where or how you grew up, your earlier aspirations and what you've done to overcome obstacles, how you created opportunities for yourself and what you are passionate, curious and enthusiastic about achieving in your life.

This is your interpretation of your life story.

You don't need to share this story at this point, but in the future, you will use this story to create your compelling message of leadership as you assist and support others toward changing, learning and growing into their leadership vision.

Leaders tell stories. As a leader, you have a story to share with others to inspire and create your leadership presence.

Write your story and file it in your leadership portfolio.

# Learning from Peer Experiences

## Who can you learn from?

If you:

- ✓ Want to learn about a new topic

- ✓ Have few resources

- ✓ Want to learn from others mistakes and experiences

Do the following:

1. Identify three or four people (Subject Matter Experts) who have been successful in your field of endeavor.

2. Clarify what it is you are intending to accomplish.

3. You will gain more respect for your request if you can effectively articulate your goal. SME's are not there to help you figure out what it is you want. That is your job.

4. If you don't know any SME's, ask people in your social network if they can tap into their network for you.

5. Assess who you want to contact based on your topic.

6. You don't need to communicate with everyone. Choose carefully. Time is a valuable resource.

7. Prepare a list of questions.

8. Write a script. Identify who you are, what you want, and who referred you.

You can:

Place a call or send an email introducing yourself, include your networking contact if necessary and your request.

Ask for assistance and not advice.

Acknowledge the individual's area of expertise that you want to tap.

WHAT'S THE MOTIVATION FOR THE SME? WHAT DO THEY GAIN FROM TAKING THE TIME TO SHARE THEIR EXPERTISE WITH YOU?

Schedule a thirty to forty-five minute meeting in a location that is convenient for the SME.

A phone conversation is sufficient. Most of the time, face-to-face meetings are difficult to schedule.

Begin with an open-ended question to warm up and begin the conversation.

It's important to establish the credibility of the SME before you take action on what they are sharing with you. The questions are designed to elicit what you need to know.

Consider including the following questions:

*How did you go about becoming a SME?*

- This is similar to reading a bibliography of a book or a research paper. It will provide you with more leads as you seek the knowledge you need.

*Who was most influential for you?*

- Determine the SME's belief system about the topic. You may or may not agree with their conclusions.

*What was your greatest lesson learned?*

- Determine if the SME is using someone else's knowledge or if it was based on their hard-earned experience.

*What, if anything, would you do differently if you had to go about it today?*

- How reflective is your SME? How up-to-date is their thinking on the topic?

*What would you continue to do if you had to do it all over again?*

- Again, determine how reflective the SME is and how valid their knowledge is concerning your topic.

*How did the experience change your perspective?*

- Is the SME thinking more broadly or more narrow in scope?

*If you were me, who should I talk with next or use as a resource?*

- It doesn't hurt to tap their resource pool.

# Acknowledge Assistance

Thank the SME for their time and send a thank you note either on personalized notepaper or via email.

Acknowledge their assistance and openness to sharing their knowledge and wisdom in a thoughtful and carefully written note.

## START USING THE KNOWLEDGE GAINED

Once you've gathered your data begin the process of assessing what is relevant to your project.

Discard anything that isn't adding value. Remain focused on what it is you desire to accomplish right now.

While you are in the middle of learning and implementing the knowledge, it's important for you to check in from time to time with a few of your SME's to determine whether or not you are:

- ✓ Heading in the right direction

- ✓ Have the appropriate information

- ✓ Not acting on previous assumptions that may not be relevant to your task

It's important to take into consideration that you may have tried something similar and experienced failure. As a result, you may carry over certain biases, feelings or emotions into the situation.

What you may not realize is that those very same biases may have contributed to your failure. Ensure you aren't on the path to creating a self-fulfilling prophecy.

# Learning As A Community Effort

IDENTIFY WHO ELSE WANTS TO LEARN THE TOPIC

Find someone else who is trying to learn the same things that you are and trade experiences.

CREATE A SMALL COMMUNITY OF LEARNERS

Consider forming a learning team or buddy group. Create a schedule for your meetings so that you can motivate each other to achieve goals.

SHARE RESOURCES WITH OTHERS INTERESTED IN LEARNING

Exchange books and other relevant resources such as websites, networking groups and associations with one another.

BE A LEADER

These things rarely work without some type of leadership.
Here is an opportunity to be in leadership regarding the subject you want to learn.

BE AN EXPERT. BE KNOWN FOR SOMETHING. BE A RESOURCE

It is also an opportunity to become a subject matter expert. Once you have successfully implemented your goal, people will begin to call on you for support and resources.

Be available for others. Keep the knowledge and wisdom flowing and you will be rewarded when others share with you.

# Learning From the Lessons of Others

What works well when "learning from others"?

BENEFITS

People generally report:

- It was relevant to something I was trying to complete at the time.

- The person took the time to answer my questions.

- I had time to practice.

- I wasn't frightened of being humiliated but felt relaxed and calm.

- Everyone was in the same situation as me. I wasn't the only person trying to do this.

Conduct a web search to determine what resources are available that could help jumpstart your learning journey, including communities with similar interests and passions.

Keep a daily or weekly journal or diary to document your thoughts, feelings, concerns and challenges.

# Identify What it is You Need to Do to Continue Learning

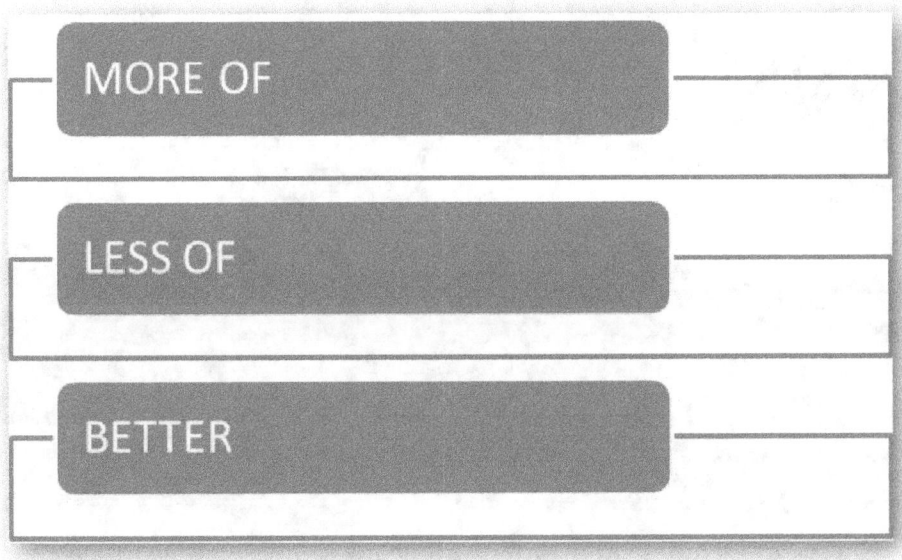

You may discover some things that are outside of the goal and timeframe you created for achievement.

In order to stay on track, but not lose the data, indicate in your framework what's relevant to your goal and what isn't.

# Prioritize Learning Activities

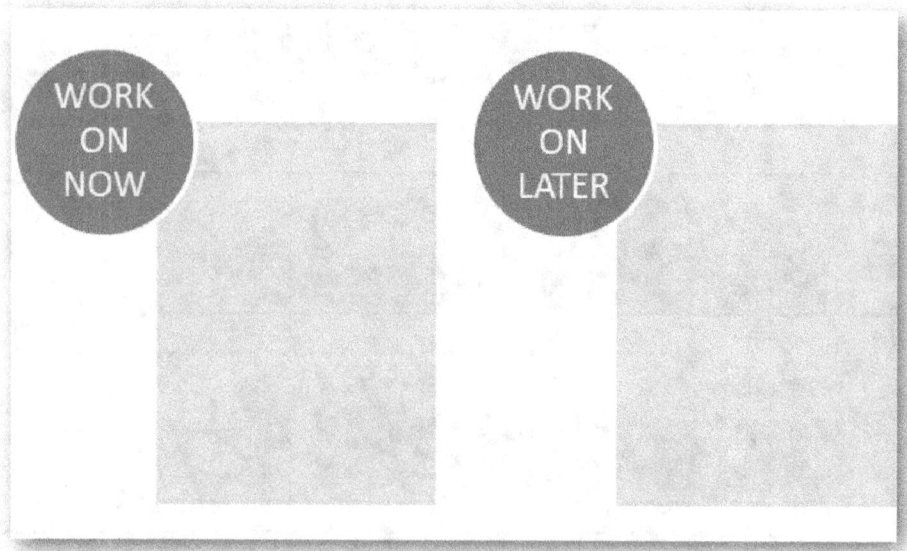

# How to Help Groups Learn to be Better Collaborators

---

Setting up meaningful group learning activities can be a great boon to enabling change in any environment.

There are numerous benefits of group learning activities if there is an intention to grow and develop the individual members. The benefits are numerous. Members will:

- ✓ Gain wisdom and perspective that is different than their own

- ✓ Develop tolerance and respect for diversity of opinion

- ✓ Develop tolerance for failure as a necessary ingredient when an outcome is not assured and the path taken is new and relatively untested. So long as failure is not the end game, you aren't experiencing anything different from anyone else. The important thing is to learn from the failure.

- ✓ Foster longer-term thinking

## Guidelines

Establish a few Guiding Principles for meetings:

- Agree to build a trusted, reliable, committed, passionate and curious group of individuals who have a common aspiration of achieving goals, sharing knowledge and information.

- Build the group with individuals who believe that together they are more powerful than acting alone in their learning experience.

- Articulate the values that the group holds as contributing to each member and to the group.

- Create ground rules for the norms and rules – what is acceptable/unacceptable behavior during meetings and for specific tasks.

# How to Help Teams Learn Together

---

This is an activity which, when conducted over time, can increase the value of your results because of the accumulated experiences and knowledge you've gained as you apply what worked and what didn't work to the next activity. Your ability to learn will increase and your performance will improve.

The activity works with individuals as well as groups and teams of people who have been working on an activity or a project together.

It's important to determine what it was that you intended to achieve as a result of the activity.

## Ask:

- What was supposed to happen as a result of my efforts?

- What actually happened when I took action?

- What happened to cause the difference between what I intended and what resulted?

- What should I do differently the next time so that I get closer to the result I want to achieve?

- What could have gone better?

If you are conducting this activity for yourself, allow 15 minutes to complete and document the results.

For teams, allow for 30 minutes and ensure that everyone understands the expectations and intended outcomes of the discussion.

# About Change

Successful change efforts require Leadership at all levels, Education and knowledge of what's expected, Communications of what's working and not working, and Measurement of intended results.

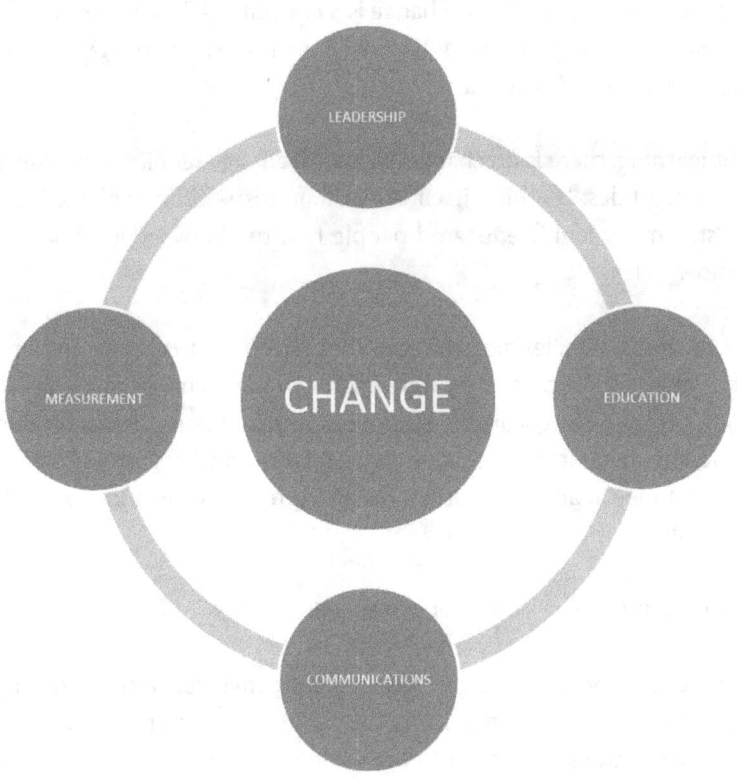

# Change Management As A Leadership Skill

INTRODUCTION: A RECAP OF HOW LEARNING AND CHANGE ARE INTEGRATED

As most people are aware, change is a constant. A key leadership skill is the ability to change, adapt and grow. But in order to change, a leader must possess the ability to learn.

Without learning, there is no change. Nearly all change requires new skill-sets, behaviors or attitudes. Learning itself is a skill and is seldom explained or taught. Further still, many highly educated people lack the knowledge of how to teach people how to learn.

Many a business, families and communities have failed to grow and enrich the lives of its members because they were unable to learn, change and grow together. They didn't know how to learn together so that their vision, goals and values could withstand the inevitable process of change. Decay and disillusionment resulted rather than renewal and transformation into a more viable and vibrant business or community.

Their communities were no longer sustainable.

An example that most people can relate to is a convenience store they must frequently use or visit. Time after time, the same mistakes are made by mindless and repetitive actions that result in the same outcomes. You get the feeling that everyone is brain-dead in the place. You wonder to yourself in amazement and frustration, "Can't these people ever learn?"

Imagine this scenario played out in the numerous institutions, organizations and bureaucracies you must frequent in order to live in your community. It is rare that the average person doesn't, at least once a day, shake their head in amazement at all of the stupid and ignorant things they witness every day.

We are all guilty of ignorance. Sometimes the act of learning can feel like an up-hill battle. Of all the attributes that differentiate effective from ineffective action, learning is a key contributor to success or failure.

Most of the time people are performing their tasks without benefit of reflection or taking a step back to identify, examine and analyze what has worked and why and what hasn't worked and why not.

Learning and possessing the know how to teach others to learn are key leadership attributes. It is the only way the leader will be able to sustain any gains they may have achieved through their best efforts.

# When Leading Change: Education and Communication

## KEY DRIVERS

People need information and knowledge with regard to the change they are implementing. Otherwise they will be confused, paralyzed and unable to move forward.

For people who are acting from your leadership or guidance it will be essential to do the following:

1. Understand the risks and rewards of the change and communicate them clearly in compelling messages.

2. Commit to an energizing and engaging vision of change. Your own enthusiasm and excitement will inspire people to get on board with the change.

3. Paint a picture of the vision for change that others can understand.

Be patient and tolerant of others ability to learn and grow with the change. They will not have the benefit of knowing precisely what your vision is unless you continually communicate your ideas and plans and engage them in a dialogue, which is inclusive, empowering, caring and compassionate.

A leader must pay careful attention to the following:

- Clearly identify what it is that you expect. Carefully explain what the individual's role is in the change process.

- Ensure that individuals have the information and knowledge needed to take first steps. Provide sufficient education and consistent and timely communication through the change.

- Identify expectations of yourself and others. Be realistic and continue to guard against overreach, self-fulfilling prophecies, and making assumptions about your environment.

- Understand what the boundaries are between the commitment of others and your own determination to implement the goal.

- Provide support in helping your stakeholders deal with the natural resistance to change including fear and discomfort of having to learn something new.

- Provide a safe environment for learning while understanding that no one likes to look bad, be wrong or humiliate themselves in front of others.

- Remember that learning takes time and big change won't happen quickly.

- Engage stakeholders in identifying ways to measure progress.

- Celebrate successes along the way.

- Don't withhold praise for fear that people will get comfortable. Understand that way of thinking is a myth learned from others who only knew one way to create and manage change.

Remember that all learning involves change. No learning, no change. It is only burdensome when the leader is in reactive mode, always putting out brush fires and never planning for the inevitability of having to deal with challenges.

S elf-fulfilling prophecies can make or break the execution of any vision and sabotage any change.

WHAT IS A SELF-FULFILLING PROPHECY?

Human beings are in a constant state of judging, forming opinions, making generalizations and pre-assessing situations. This is normal.

Survival instincts and our hard-wiring predispose us to think ahead of our opponents, consider who or what may threaten our existence or how to conserve energy, resources and will-power.

It is not a fault of the human character but how it is that we are still standing after a few thousand years of existence.

Once again, the tools and resources that enhanced the human being's survival rate were appropriate in an age when life held many physical threats such as encountering a hungry tiger, poisonous snake or other enemy.

## That was the past.

In today's world, prejudging a situation without testing assumptions can threaten a successful outcome just as harshly as a surprised bear could remove one of your limbs.

Authentic leadership holds you to a higher standard and requires that you transcend the bare essentials of survival.

Relying on instinct or intuition will help to sustain life at a survival level but those tools alone will not support growth and development beyond the cavemen and cavewomen stage.

A self-fulfilling prophecy is:

- ✓ A pre-determined set of beliefs and conclusions applied to a person or group.

- ✓ It predicts their actions and behavior based upon your own point of view and perspective.

- ✓ It is not based on experience with the individual or group or any previous behavior or actions.

- ✓ It can simply be your perspective or perceived reality.

- ✓ It is untested and generally you will be tempted to search for evidence to prove that your assumptions were correct.

Why do self-fulfilling prophecies harm or sabotage our efforts?

Oftentimes, people make generalizations and conclusions that are false.

False information does not support success and will ensure failure. Many times, this behavior will encourage people to cover up the information and to hide false assumptions that created havoc.

People don't like to be wrong and will do anything to avoid looking bad.

What can a leader do to avoid making self-fulfilling prophecies?

## Leaders can:

- Understand that making assumptions and pre-judging is normal and that no one likes to be wrong, taken by surprise or not have the answers.

- Take time and apply resources toward testing assumptions, beliefs, prejudices, judgments, and perceptions about the situation and people involved.

The change process takes time and energy.

## Do you want to disrupt or change "what is"?

Then test your assumptions so they don't become self-fulfilling prophecies.

Think about some self-fulfilling prophecies you've experienced lately. How did it turn out for you and others?

# Challenges to Change: Current Assumptions

As you create and share your plan for taking new actions toward achieving your strategic goals, you will encounter individuals who may or may not be supportive of your aspirations.

## Should you be concerned?

Yes.

Most goals require cooperation, assistance, support and the actions of others, especially if you are being in leadership in life.

It is important for you to identify and pre-determine the individuals you will engage as you take action in your environment. These individuals are called your "key stakeholders" which include influential individuals, potential investors, talented resources, advisors, board members, partners and collaborators.

## Where to begin

Begin by reviewing your goals and identifying who has a stake in helping you achieve them.

Make 3 lists:

✓   Anyone who will be involved in decision-making

✓ People who are influential in your field – sphere of influence is greater than your own such as in the investment world

✓ People who have specialized expertise, skills and competencies who can act as Advisors, Board Members

Once you have determined the individuals, assess their stake using the following questions.

- What does each individual have to gain or lose as a result of the intended outcome of the plan?

- What will motivate them to agree or disagree with what it is you want to achieve?

- How do you think they will resist or what objections may they have about your idea or proposed change?

- What might they do to thwart/help your efforts?

- How might they sabotage your efforts through intentional negative press or use of social media?

- Who will be supportive of your success and who might be an ally?

## Now, test your assumptions.

- How do you know that the assumptions you made are true about the individuals you analyzed?

- What evidence is there that any of the answers to the questions are truth and reality?

- How did you arrive at believing these answers to be true? What specifically did the individuals involved do or say to cause you to believe they would react in the same ways?

- What do you need to do differently to test your assumptions about your key stakeholders?

## Why is this a critical task?

What you are identifying is the level of resistance you think or feel the stakeholders will have with regard to the change you want to create.

It is important for a leader to understand the concept of resistance to change in a way that empowers the goal rather than challenges the effort.

Evaluating pre-determined assumptions can make the difference between success and failure of any change effort or new venture.

# Resistance To Change: Principles To Consider

Resistance to change is natural. When there is no resistance, the leader should be alert to the possibility that there may be someone or something that will arise which will attempt to sabotage or place the change in jeopardy.

## Doing Pulse Checks

- Pay careful attention to non-verbal behaviors. Don't become paranoid. Use a reasonable amount of skepticism, accepting the fact that resistance to change is a normal human condition. Even people who claim to love change will have a reaction to a new idea. Their way of resisting the new idea is to question, "Tear it apart", and try to find reasons "why it won't work" or similar behaviors. Some hide the feeling of "resistance" behind the word "feedback".

- Create communications activities, which allow for both public disclosure as well as anonymous input.

- Check in with individuals who typically have a finger on the pulse of the communities in which you are involved and who matter to your efforts.

- Graciously accept the feedback and reward versus punishing people for their honesty.

- Don't attempt to persuade people they are "wrong" or "don't understand".

- Continue to work the process; reinforce key messages; continue testing and experimenting.

- Sometimes you will just have to go with your gut; go out on a limb and do what you need to do regardless of resistance, skepticism or negativity.

There are numerous examples of change agents, entrepreneurs and leaders who have gone against the grain and were enormously successful.

# More Tips to Consider

- Don't assume that when people are quiet that they are on board with what it is that you want to create.

- Remember that you are asking people and yourself to change. How will you resist your own plan for change? Prepare for it.

- People need to be right. Change will cause people to have to learn new skills, concepts, and ways of behaving or believing.

- There is fear that they will be wrong or fail.

- Oftentimes leaders react with anger and hostility, further driving resistance deeper and deeper while creating a nearly insurmountable wall.

## You can't communicate enough

- ✓ Communicate all the ways that are available to learn that minimize the risk of failure.

- ✓ Walk the talk.

- ✓ Learn along side of others.

- ✓ Demonstrate what is new.

✓ Ask for feedback.

✓ Be honest.

## Check you are making the right assumptions

Nothing endangers change and learning more than placing judgments on people and situations without checking the assumptions upon which the "truth" was based. What we think about most has a way of controlling our own actions and behaviors and creating the results we fear most.

✓ Self-reflect

✓ Frequently request feedback

# Change and The Human Condition

eeding to be right, looking good and being in control are among a leader's deadliest enemies.

## That may sound like a shocking statement.

It is not.

These enemies live within the leader's own psyche and must be dealt with on a daily basis.

They tend to kill feedback and criticism, setting people up to fail, and create a wall of defensiveness that cannot be penetrated.

New knowledge cannot enter the wall built by these enemies. New learning cannot occur, as the mind is too busy defending what it already knows how to do well.

Past success can become the breeding ground for future failure.

Many of the leaders WE DO NOT ADMIRE fall into this very human trap.

They show up as:

Command and Control bosses

Micromanagers

Paranoid Dictators

If you are fearful of becoming this type of Leader, you will need to be MINDFUL of the human condition and what lurks inside of you.

- Stay aware and self-conscious.

- Be honest with yourself.

- Acknowledge where you need to be resilient, adaptive, open and as non-judging as possible.

Everyone judges. What makes the difference is how much and with what frequency we judge both ourselves and others.

# Tips Important Enough to Repeat

## HOW TO MANAGE RESISTANCE TO CHANGE

- Accept that resistance is a natural reaction to change.

- Empathize with your stakeholders, audience or individuals who will be affected by your change.

- Identify your stakeholders' concerns by asking open-ended questions. Don't attempt to advocate or persuade for a particular position. Instead, inquire into what it is people are attracted to and may fear that they will lose as a result of this change.

- Understand your own biases, opinions, beliefs and assumptions about the stakeholders, audience and individuals you are addressing with the change you want to create.

- Identify what the "gain" or benefit is for each of your key stakeholders. Every individual or group has its own stake in the change – what's in it for them?

- Have the courage to hear people's concerns without fear that once heard or acknowledged the responses will become reasons for not changing. Hold yourself accountable to a higher standard of behaving.

- Know what the "comfort zone" is for people involved in the change and what the risks are that they will need to incur in order to move forward in the direction of the change.

- Identify and acknowledge the price you are willing to pay to have the change occur.

It is natural for people to desire to preserve and protect their own way of doing things even if those behaviors, attitudes and activities maintain a status quo that is no longer viable.

Oftentimes, people will not want to expose what they feel is their ignorance and will shy away from talking with a potential role model or mentor. That is why it is important to feel the tension between what you want and where you are now – keeping your vision or goal in clear line of sight. It will help to get you over your natural fears and concerns and allow you to pay the costs to achieve your dreams.

The more you do to keep the payoff in sight, the greater your motivation will be.

## Focus on the emotional side of change

As a leader, you know the importance of having a powerful set of tools to empower and assist others in learning, growing and changing.

The following is a set of guidelines for acknowledging and tending to the emotional side of change.

1.  Help people find personal meaning and value in what is being requested of them.

2.  Allow for time, care and a positive intention to take the place of platitudes, slogans and mantra.

3.  Pay attention to your language – it needs to be in integrity with how and what it is that you are requesting. Sometimes the leader must find a new language, one they may not be familiar with or comfortable using. But if the change is to create a different world, a different language is necessary to explain what the new vision is.

4.  Respect that people change at different rates and not everyone will immediately jump on board and embrace it.

5.  Create meaningful, measurable steps so that everyone knows how well the change is progressing.

6.  Listen carefully to feedback and respect what is heard; translate the feedback into meaningful actions and new behaviors

How will you apply these guidelines to your change effort?

Continue to incorporate new information and knowledge as you forge your leadership identity, developing your vision, taking new actions and practicing new behaviors.

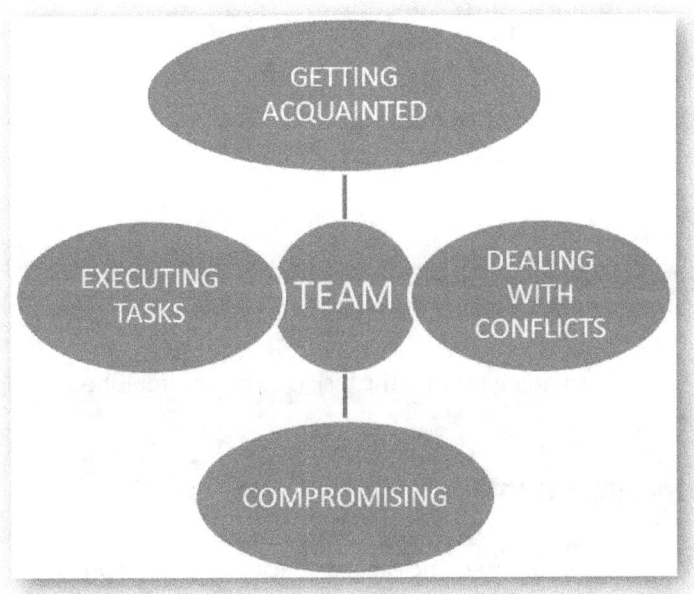

## TEAMS WORK THROUGH A PROCESS BEFORE THEY CAN EFFECTIVELY FUNCTION

First, they strive to get to know one another and assess strengths, weaknesses, level of commitment to goals and willingness to do the work.

Second, they oftentimes get to the point where they disagree and/or engage in conflict.

Third, with a healthy team, they will settle down into a normal routine of work and engage with one another in order to be productive and achieve goals.

# How To Form A Strong, Collaborative And High-Functioning Team

During the early formation of a team, it's important for the leader, change agent or individuals who take up a leadership role to help the group to work with:

✓ A clear set of goals

✓ Ground rules for how they will work together

✓ An understanding of what the task is to be accomplished

## Why is this important?

In a shocking number of cases, unclear goals, lack of a mindful process of how best to work together and unfamiliarity with the information being addressed is how teams exist.

This is the case whether it is a graduate school project, business project or entrepreneurial venture.

If the groundwork is not carefully laid at the beginning of the project or collaboration, a team can flounder for a long time in endless debate over who is right and who is wrong. Oftentimes, individual team members will have differing opinions of what the actual goal is and how to go about achieving it.

Keeping in mind the following points can be helpful.

People have different styles that include:

Conflict Resolution

Decision-Making

Problem-Solving

Learning

Managing Time and Prioritizing

Organization

Planning

Oftentimes people don't realize these styles are actual skill-sets as well and fall under the category of "management".

Management has come to be known as a ROLE rather than a set of skills to organize, plan, evaluate, analyze and a host of other competencies necessary for implementing goals, missions and simply getting a product or service to market.

Everything we do in service of getting something done involves these management skills and competencies.

**Management is a process of DOING
Versus
Leadership is a way of BEING.**

Mix in personality characteristics, brain wiring and simple preferences. You can easily see why it is challenging to accomplish goals in highly complex, ever-changing environments.

Technology creates efficiencies of scale.

Human beings must still manage and lead efforts, decide which tools make the most sense and help themselves and others learn new methods on a continuous basis.

Spending an appropriate amount of time upfront will create considerably better outcomes for all involved.

# Begin Teamwork with a Good Process

1. A team should reflect upon and formulate responses to the following questions:

   What are we here to do?

2. Set a specific amount of time to answer this question before moving on to the next set of questions.

   - How shall we organize ourselves?
   - Who is the leader or facilitator?
   - Who cares about our success? Our failure?
   - How do we work through our problems?
   - What challenges might we face? How should we handle them?
   - How do we fit with other groups?
   - What benefits do team members need from the team?

# How to Facilitate Effective Group Conversation

## DO'S AND DON'TS

Pay attention to the bigger picture perspective; help others do the same.

Refrain from taking a position early on; it will squelch honesty and fair debate of the issues.

Rephrase what you think you heard; explore other thought processes with honesty, objectivity and consistency.

Refrain from disregarding your own feelings, values and insights.

Determine whether you can arrive at conclusions that move beyond validating your own position.

Examine your assumptions that led to a current position.

Allow your opinions to be influenced by others – encourage your assumptions to be challenged by others.

Practice self-disclosure – how you arrived at a position, what led to the thinking and how it may have affected others.

Examine where you may have taken a defensive position and ask yourself:

- What was the situation?  Reflect upon what happened as a result.

- How did you behave under the circumstances that were occurring?

- Were you pleased with the outcome?

- If you weren't satisfied, what might you have said or done differently to realize a different outcome?

- How would that have affected the result of the discussion?

- What can you take away from the experience that would benefit you in the future?

- If you were to have an opportunity to share this experience, what lessons would you communicate? What did you learn that others could benefit from your experience?

# How to Conduct An Effective Meeting

- Assign an individual the role of timekeeper; establish a system of rotation so that everyone has an opportunity and responsibility for keeping the momentum going.

- Identify a few goals that can be accomplished within a reasonable timeframe.

- Conduct individual audits that represent the collective knowledge and wisdom of the network.

- Identify gaps – where the network needs additional resources or other stakeholders who can be tapped for specific knowledge and information.

- Establish a place to keep documents relative to the needs of the network.

- Have a clear intention that everyone knows and understands, allowing for individual visions.

- Determine whether or not it makes sense to develop a network project that members can use as a pilot or proto-type for future learning together.

- Facilitate a "question and answer" period to determine what worked well and what didn't work during the meeting; incorporate what was learned in the next meeting and in your guiding principles.

# How to Evaluate Effective Teamwork

This activity can be used after team meetings to help the individual members reflect on what took place during the time spent on a particular topic.

As a leader, you are promoting the idea of reflection that leads to learning. You can use the tool to establish a context for a conversation that holds everyone accountable and responsible for creating results.

Too often, individuals will talk about how ineffective a meeting was after the fact rather than at a time when action can be taken to course-correct.

Applying after action reviews signals the team that participation in meetings is key and their performance will be rewarded according to the quality of their input and ideas.

Complete the following statements:

1.  My participation as a team member so far has been:

2.  The degree to which my ideas have been listened to by other team members is:

3.  The degree to which the team is really working together is:

4.  My satisfaction with my membership in this team is:

5.  Based on our level of teamwork today, I predict the rating of our teamwork two months from now will be:

# How to Conduct a Team Meeting Debrief

This tool can be used to assist a team in conducting further evaluation of their planning process. It is essential to have an activity in place which supports the behavior of adjusting, improving and course-correcting your mission or goal achievement.

What's working/what's not working?

What can we do more of?

What can we discontinue doing?

How effective have our strategies been to date?

Are our strategies getting us the desired results?

Are we gaining ground on the result or are we coasting in place?

What will move us closer to the results?

What happens to us when things don't go as we expected?

Do we re-group, discuss and take an honest account of what we have been doing?

Or, do we continue on the same path, hoping for a breakthrough?

How do we typically handle obstacles? Do our attitudes and behaviors help or hinder us?

Are there any team members who are not pulling their weight?

How do we address these sensitive issues?

Who can help us facilitate a process to handle upsets the team may be experiencing?

How do we handle the time gap between actions and results?

What are our constraints?

How do we feel about the leadership of the team?

What changes do we need to make in order to ensure our success?

# About Being a Mentor

# About Being a Mentor

THE LEADERSHIP TASK IS A PROCESS THAT IS FACILITATED AT AN APPROPRIATE PACE THAT IS COMFORTABLE FOR THE INDIVIDUAL BEING MENTORED.

IT IS ALSO THE RESPONSIBILITY OF THE MENTEE TO COMPLETE THE TASKS, INTEGRATE THE MENTOR'S INSIGHTS AND TAKE FULL RESPONSIBILITY FOR THE OUTCOMES OF THE MEETINGS.

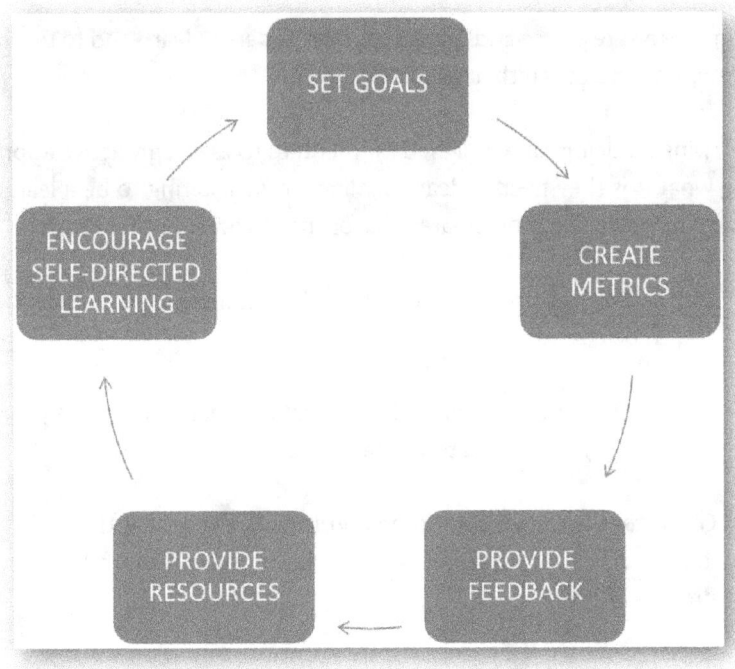

# Leaders As Mentors

A powerful change tool is mentorship. One-on-one assistance to customize a learning/action plan for individual development is one of the surest ways to enable success during change or help someone through a steep learning curve.

Leaders engage in mentoring others as they learn and grow.

It is an important resource and critical tool for leaders to learn and to teach others how to mentor and coach their protégés.

The following guidelines are designed for mentees to take a proactive approach to learning what it is they need to learn. An individual aspiring to be a leader in life finds out what is needed and creates approaches to achieve their goals.

- ✓ Don't wait for someone else to take the initiative to reach out and invite you to be coached.

- ✓ Take charge and determine who or what it is that can provide you with an opportunity to accelerate your ability to learn.

- ✓ Given that learning takes time and time is a resource that is in increasingly short supply, you will need to use effective tools to help you in the process of learning.

A leader can share an enormous amount of knowledge in the form of tips, strategies and guidelines for those undertaking or undergoing change.

# About Meetings

# About Meetings

**IMPORTANT MEETING TASKS INCLUDE THE FOLLOWING:**

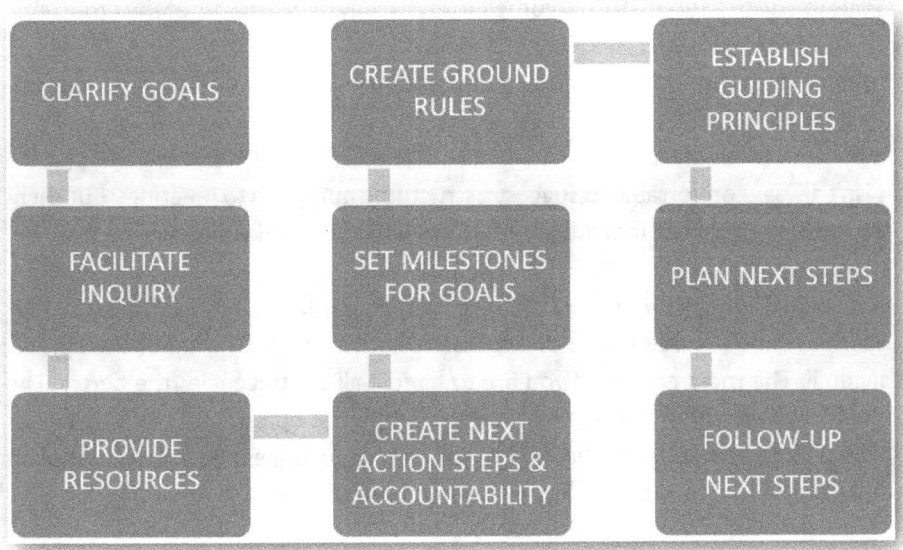

| | | |
|---|---|---|
| CLARIFY GOALS | CREATE GROUND RULES | ESTABLISH GUIDING PRINCIPLES |
| FACILITATE INQUIRY | SET MILESTONES FOR GOALS | PLAN NEXT STEPS |
| PROVIDE RESOURCES | CREATE NEXT ACTION STEPS & ACCOUNTABILITY | FOLLOW-UP NEXT STEPS |

# How to Set Ground Rules for Effective Meetings

f you are leading a meeting or developing the agenda for one, use these ground rules to quickly initiate a dialogue with the team about the most effective methods to create a successful outcome for your meeting regardless of the group size.

Establish and agree upon a set of ground rules that will go a long way toward creating a successful outcome.

It isn't always comfortable to suggest a structured approach to meetings. But there are meetings between individuals or groups where the stakes are high.

Professional groups hire mediators, negotiators and facilitators. You may not always have the luxury of time or expense to undertake the hiring of such an individual. The more equipped you are to handle all contingencies the better. The more knowledgeable you are regarding the proper set up, structure and dynamics of an effective meeting, the better you will be able to judge the effectiveness of an individual who makes their living providing these services.

Pay attention to the bigger picture perspective

Refrain from taking a position early on

Rephrase what you think you heard

Explore with honesty, objectivity and consistency

Refrain from disregarding your own feelings, values and insights

See if you can arrive at conclusions that move beyond validating your own position

Examine the assumptions that led to a current position

Establish a place to keep documents relative to the needs of the network

Have a clear intention that everyone knows and understands, allowing for individual visions

Determine whether or not it makes sense to develop a network project that members can use as a pilot or proto-type for future learning together

Conduct an after action review to determine what worked well and didn't work well during the meeting; incorporate the lessons learned in the next meeting and in the guiding principles

# In Summary

---

# Practicing New Behaviors Takes Time and Energy

Practice is important, especially if you are learning a new behavior for the first time. Knowing you may not achieve one hundred percent of your goal will help you set realistic expectations.

CELEBRATE SMALL WINS

It's important to celebrate small successes and reward yourself for your efforts.

DO TIMELY PULSE CHECKS

Stay in tune with emotions that you have during the first stage of learning something new. Oftentimes, people feel uncomfortable when learning something new. They may be reluctant to share their goal with others for fear of ridicule, criticism or judgment.

RESIST SELF-JUDGING BEHAVIOR

The voice of judgment can be very strong especially when conditioned by years of being told what your capabilities are or what others expect of you.

Don't allow other people to set limitations on you. They are only projecting their own fears and subconsciously will not want you to succeed especially if it's something they tried to do and failed.

RELAX AND ENJOY THE JOURNEY

Be kind to yourself and know that everyone will learn at their pace. Some people need to understand the context first or the big picture. Others will focus on details and need to maintain a high level of energy and positive mental framework to keep their vision in clear sight.

MAKE YOUR VISION VISIBLE

Creating a vision board with pictures of you achieving your goals is motivating and helps to create a very positive self-fulfilling prophecy.

# Leadership Lessons

---

There will always be lessons in life to learn. Here is a list of lessons we have learned about the kind of leaders we aspire to always be.

#1      Leaders live on purpose.

#2      Leaders make choices based on a vision or goals they create for where they want to be and what it is they want to be doing.

#3      Leaders own who they be in the world. No excuses.

#4      Leaders plan, do, think, course correct, pay attention to what they and others are feeling, how they are impacting those around them including their communities and environment.

#5      Leaders identify and live their values.

#6      Leaders initiate, take stands and risk not looking good, not being right, and not always being in control.

#7      Leaders pay a price for what they believe in.

#8      Leaders never rest on their laurels or take being a leader for granted. They are always in a state of learning, evolving, changing and growing.

# Quotes for Inspiration

---

The following quotes are excerpts from the book, "Leadership – Creating a Path, Leaving a Mark" by Jo Singel, 2008

*Leadership is timeless.*

*Leadership takes time.*

*Leadership is a process, a path, a journey and most important, of all, a choice.*

*You choose leadership; leadership doesn't choose you.*

*Leadership is open to everyone, at every level and has no limits as to who is a leader.*

*Leadership is a solitary path yet it involves having an impact on others.*

*Leaders reflect on their contribution, impact and legacy.*

*Leaders make mistakes; they know that is the way to learn.*

*Leaders grow, share and care.*

*Leaders blaze a path many others don't take. They never stop searching and scanning their inner and outer environments. Sometimes they need to take the high ground and create the vision in their own mind before they share it with the world.*

*Courtesy of Jonathan Singel*

*A leader can observe from many different angles.*

*What looks the same to most people offers numerous possibilities to the leader.*

*A leader is a hunter and planner knowing there are times when the pursuit of the goal requires focus and perseverance.*

It's always about the subtle contrasts.

Some perspectives or views have more light than others.

Leaders seek the bright spots, however dim on the horizon they may be.

They will sit and wait out the storms, knowing that they always

pass even when they may leave destruction in their path.

Leaders pick themselves up and get to work on the plan to

shed light on the dark areas and look for opportunities

even when the prospects appear to be dim and remote.

Leaders keep the light in themselves knowing that life

can interrupt any view: sunny, bright or dark.

*Leaders decide which paths are worth pursuing. Some paths are easier to*

*follow than others. Does that mean those with challenges*

*shouldn't be pursued? Are they worth the work?*

*All paths have uncertain futures. Which ones to take and when*

*are always questions for the leader.*

*Sometimes people live in environments and circumstances*

*that are difficult to overcome with pithy platitudes and positive thinking.*

*What helps those individuals aspire to be in leadership in life and in their communities?*

*How deep is the pain that prevents the individual from climbing*

*beyond where they are to where they could be?*

*There are no easy answers. No one said that leadership was easy.*

*Things get old and they decay. That is the cycle of life and death.*

*Unavoidable. Yet, while we are here there are so many things*

*we can do to recreate and revitalize what's important...*

*Things change. Always. Sometimes for the better; sometimes for the worse.*

*But change they will. Who we "be" when things change will make*

*all the difference in what we "do" and what we create as a result.*

Sometimes you just have to hit the pause button and take a hard look at yourself.

We can take ourselves a little too seriously sometimes.

There are days when I wish I were a shadow lightly touching what is around me.

That way I wouldn't make any mistakes.

And then I remind myself of who I am and why I'm here.

*Leaders are almost always bridge builders.*

*They notice what's missing and find ways to solve problems.*

*Leaders can be very practical.*

*Yet they always have a "big picture" in mind.*

*The Verrazano Bridge in New York City was a vision that was beautifully realized.*

*Leaders take the long view but also see the details.*

*Achieving satisfaction from completed goals gains*

*you a new perspective from which to continue to set*

*and achieve progressively challenging and bigger goals.*

*What is important now?*

# Leadership Stories

# A CEO

---

Consider a case where the CEO of a Fortune 200 company has oversight for the lives of thousands if not hundreds of thousands of people in a country other than his own. This is a true situation. The company lost a key military defense contract. Thousands of people were employed in a plant far from the continent where this CEO managed the organization. There was a great deal of pressure from the management team and the Board of Directors to close the plant where these people worked. There would be no work for a very long time. There was no contract that would provide a very large number of people with earning a viable living.

The CEO had to make the final decision. He was very distressed and torn about whether or not to close the plant. But he had to do it. Otherwise, the entire company including its fortunes and future would be at stake.

The plant closed and four thousand people were displaced.

The CEO openly wept over the decision. But it had to be done. He was in a business where he was responsible to the entire organization. Even though he regarded the business as a family institution, he was answerable to the board of directors, the Wall Street analysts and the shareholders of the company.

The CEO took responsibility for the overall health and welfare of the organization regardless of his personal feelings for the individuals involved.

If you were the CEO what would you or could you have done differently, if anything?

Do you believe he was justified in his actions or might there have been other alternatives?

If you were his second in command what questions might you have asked or approaches taken?

What would you do if you were the individual in the leadership role in a similar situation where people's livelihoods were at stake?

# A Story About Mary

Mary, a corporate professional decides to take stock of her life and complete a lifeline.

What she discovers is that when certain people were in her life she felt more content and fulfilled in what she was doing. For Mary, strong and caring relationships coincided with success in her job. Conversely, when Mary was feeling alone and alienated from family and friends, her career took a downhill slide and she found herself in a situation where she felt she had to start over again. After Mary completed her lifeline she concluded that her value for nurturing and authentic relationships were a top priority. In the future, she would ensure that no matter how hectic her career became she would plan time to attend family gatherings, have dinners with good friends and not lose touch as she pursued her professional goals.

This is the value of taking time to examine and assess people, places and events taking place over the course of time and the significance they may have held.

Perhaps you met an individual who became a mentor and you discovered things about yourself that you would not have otherwise noticed.

This may be an indication that at certain times you need to cultivate certain types of relationships and place yourself into situations that are unfamiliar and even uncomfortable.

It is easy to slide into the drift of life and not notice that you are far from where you wanted to be.

Sometimes an unfamiliar place can act as a challenge for you to explore different aspects of your talents and aspirations.

You may also discover that a retreat or workshop you took had a powerful effect and that you recreated yourself as a result.

Whether it be a person, a place, an event or a thing it's important to understand your own particular motivators and how to seek them out, nurture them and incorporate them into your life.

# A Story About Don

Consider the story of Don who, as a young man grew up in a small steel mill town in a mountainous and isolated area of Pennsylvania far away from any large city. The chief source of entertainment was high school football teams, movies in the one cinema on Main Street and for the elders, the local tap room where stories and punches were frequently exchanged especially around the time the weekly paycheck was cashed.

For the most part, people in the town there were poor. The town had a right and wrong side of the tracks where the better off could compare themselves to those who had less than they did. The houses were square wooden boxes placed closely together on levels that went higher and higher up the mountain upon which the town was built. Because of the day and night operation of the steel mill, there was a persistent red dust that covered every car, fence and house within a ten mile radius. People mingled on the Main Street where food, clothing and the occasional trinket were purchased. Despite the poverty, life was stable, families were strong and for the most part no one starved to death. Beggars on the streets were simply non-existent.

His mother and father decided, as good parents will do, to relocate the family in order to achieve a higher standard of living. Don's father worked hard to educate himself. He raised himself up from steel-mill worker to head of a music department in a school in a middle-class neighborhood miles from his hometown.

Don could have easily followed in his father's footsteps. Himself a gifted musician, he could have continued as a respectable citizen in the town where his family was known and he had built strong ties and good friendships. But as the years passed, Don began to formulate a dream of his own. Always a strong and independent child who took his life in his own hands, upon graduation he joined the Air Force, left home and never returned except to visit.

Don's experience of life was far different from his parents. While in the Air Force, his exposure to different people and new ideas motivated him to dream a bigger dream - to live and work in New York City.

Don was an intelligent young man with strong interpersonal skills. At an early age he was personable, charismatic, persuasive, kind and caring. He made friends easily and people wanted to know him wherever he went. He worked hard at his job, took responsibility for whatever task he embarked upon and before long he was living and working in Manhattan, managing people in a respectable corporate position.

Why is Don's story in a book about leadership? The meaning of Don's story is that, from the time he was a young boy and growing into young manhood, Don had a strong sense of self. Was he always on track with his goals? No. Did he always do the right and correct thing? No. But what he did was to continue to follow his heart, questioning the "rightness" of the situation he was in and whether or not it served him and others in positive ways.

Today, Don is a husband, father and manager in a position where his job is to help others learn, grow and develop themselves into their best selves regardless of their beginnings, resources and/or current skills. He does his work with passion and the assuredness of someone who has empathy for others' circumstances, their capacity to learn and their willingness to do the work.

Don is a leader of his life. He is a mentor, coach, and role model for others who strive to create their own path in life, relying upon themselves as their own best teachers and forging a leadership identity that is unique, powerful and impactful. Don carries himself in a way that others think he is man who is a wealthy individual who occupies a powerful position in the world of business. Don is unique. He has never been wealthy nor does he occupy a position of great power and authority. But within himself he is both.

# A Story About Carmen

Carmen was born in a small town outside of Naples, Italy. This fact would haunt him for half of his lifetime. Carmen was never comfortable with his heritage. Growing up in an Italian-American ghetto with barely enough food to eat or clothing to wear to school, he had a self-consciousness about him that his siblings did not possess. He got into trouble along the way but was never imprisoned.

At the age of eighteen he joined the Army and was immediately drafted into World War II. The only problem was that, still denying his birthplace, he lied on his application that he was born in America. Fortunately for him, the Army was looking for any able bodied man to fight in the war. Carmen was naturalized and shipped overseas for three hard years of heavy fighting. He returned to America at the end of the war injured, with his purple heart and other medals in hand. He married the woman he left three years before and began his career as a Laborer in the U.S. Government.

Never having graduated from High School, Carmen made his way up through the ranks and joined the Department of Navy as a Firefighter for their naval ammunitions bases. A few years later he became Chief and from there on he held positions of leadership and authority.

In the evenings Carmen studied hard to learn the fundamentals of engineering and chemistry. He taught many individuals with much higher levels of education. The only reason he retired was a severe back problem that kept him hunched over in pain for the remainder of his life.

When Carmen passed away in his early sixties, he left a legacy of respect, power, self-confidence, presence, discipline, accomplishment and a family who honored him. No one would ever doubt this man's commitment and dedication. He was honest, hard-working and had a high regard for any individual he met. Carmen was a self-created man.

# You are the Hero

As the hero in your own life story, how do your values withstand the tests that come your way? Do you acquiesce easily when pressured? Or do you stay true to yourself?

We wouldn't have much regard for a hero in any story that gives up too soon in the plot.

What we expect is that our heroes never give up even if they are frequently prone to temptation. The human foibles and weaknesses keep us interested. We are eager to discover how the characters handle the challenges and will oftentimes root for the underdog if they demonstrate sufficient courage. We expect the hero will struggle. Otherwise there would be no story but merely a bland acting out of ordinary daily routines. The more difficult the challenge the more interested we are in knowing what will happen next. It will keep us glued to our seats. It will be a book we can't put down or a movie we will watch again and again for its excitement, energy and empowering messages.

Does your life story empower others with its lessons learned, risks undertaken and opportunities seized?

As the hero of your life story what does your character – what others see or experience about you – communicate or project out to the world?

Say the following phrases aloud while standing in front of a mirror. What does the person looking back at you communicate? Do you recognize confidence or fear? Does the person come across as self-assured or timid and uncertain? Practice until you get the result you want.

What does it mean when you can say to yourself?

I am committed.

I am responsible.

I persevere.

I am courageous.

I am tenacious.

I am honest.

I am trustworthy.

I respect others.

Take up your notebook once again. You are now ready to reflect upon what kind of leader you aspire to be. Or, if you do consider yourself to be a leader in life, then this is a time to consider an opportunity to re-energize yourself.

Write a story with you as the hero. What is the situation? What challenge does the hero face in the story? How do they deal with dilemmas? What motivates the hero to take action regardless of the dangers and risks?

Do you recognize yourself in this story? How close are you to realizing the vision of leadership you have for yourself? What people, places, events and things will help you to close some of the gaps or fill in the missing pieces? Consider your lifeline. Now incorporate the new information onto your map.

Now you are actively involved, with intention and strong resolve to create a future you passionately desire.

# Extra Tools

CONTINUE TO IGNITE CURIOUSITY, STIMULATE THINKING, DEVELOPING HIGHER LEVELS OF SELF-AWARENESS, WORKING ON GOALS, REFINING VISIONS AND LEARNING FROM EXPERIENCE

- ♦ **FAST TRACK ACTIONS**

- ◙ **LAUNCH IDEAS**

- ▶ **FRAMEWORKS**

- Δ **SELF-AWARENESS STIMULATOR**

- Ω **PULSE CHECKS**

► Framework

**ANALYZING BELIEFS AND ATTITUDES**

## My Beliefs and Attitudes

| Beliefs and attitudes about people, work and life | How I came to believe what I do and the attitudes I have | What beliefs and attitudes serve me in who I need and want to be |
|---|---|---|

# ◉ Launch Idea

**ACHIEVING IMPACT**

## Begin:

1. Deal with the facts of your life:
a. What is happening right now: work, home, community, family, well-being?
b. What is working; not working in each of these areas?
c. What would be an ideal situation in each of these areas?
d. Are there areas where you should change the course or direction of your current situations?
e. What are the gaps between what is and what can be?

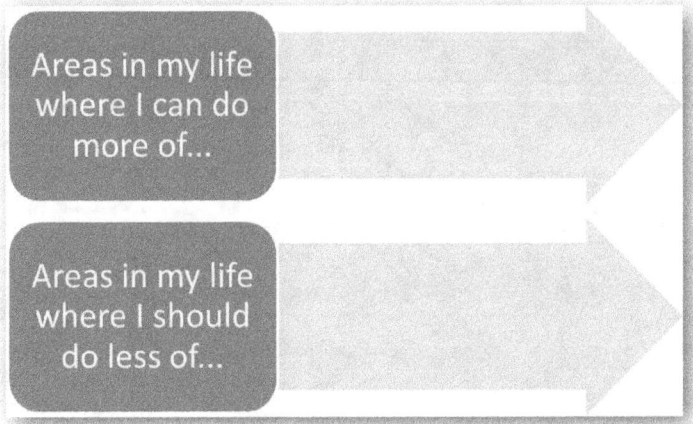

# ◆ Fast Track Action

**GETTING FEEDBACK**

1. Ask friends what they think are your best traits or talents.

2. Ask friends and/or colleagues what you can DO MORE OF, LESS OF, OR DIFFERENTLY to be a person of value.

3. Take notes about what you've learned about yourself.

4. Create 3 action steps to strengthen your qualities as an individual who others experience as a person worth knowing.

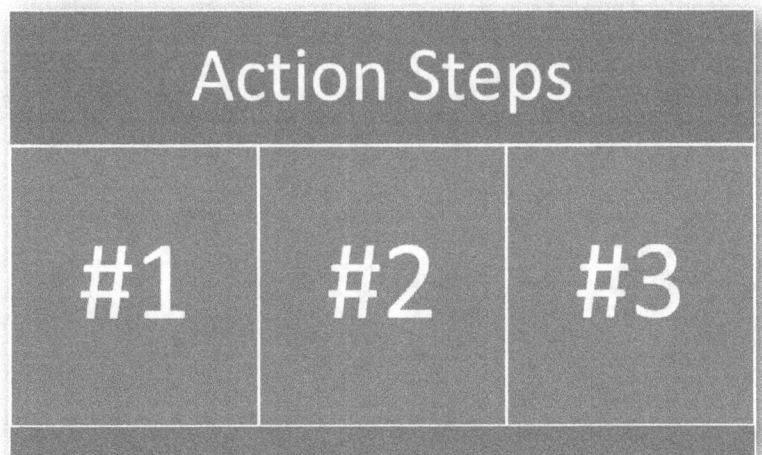

As a result of this activity, list five things you know about yourself now that you didn't know before.

1.
2.
3.
4.
5.

# △ Self-Awareness Stimulator

## Influence

Consider where you have influence right now.

Where it is you would like to have more influence?

Is it within your control?

If not, how can you explore opportunities to broaden your sphere of influence?

Who do you know who has a sphere of influence that you admire?

Set up an interview with the individual and ask them your questions.

Incorporate your answers into a plan of action.

INFLUENCE IS ABOUT HOW YOU ARE SHOWING UP IN LIFE

*Who are you? How have you been showing up in life?*

*Is it time for you to awaken to the potential within you, no matter who you currently think you are, what you think you have or what you believe you are capable of achieving?*

△ Self-Awareness Stimulator

## Decision-Making

The following incomplete sentences can help you to distinguish why you are making a decision at a particular point in time.

I feel confident when I...

I won't feel confident until I...

I feel successful when I...

I'm not happy until...

I feel loved when I...

My life is working when I...

I feel I've accomplished something when I...

My work is good when...

This is a very important discussion to have with yourself.

For some, making decisions is very stressful, involving checking in with various individuals. This typically doesn't turn out to be productive because there will not always be someone around to guide you. A good example is facing a bear in the woods. Given the number of times bears wander into local communities, it might be a good idea to practice the art of good decision making.

Sometimes, the best decision is to RUN!

# △ Self-Awareness Stimulator

## Self-Awareness

Visualize a deer standing still in the woods, sensing what is around him and taking in data through sight, sound, feel, and smell.

Awareness, as distinguished from self-awareness is a very powerful tool to practice and possess.

What can you do to enhance your awareness skills?

Take a walk in a natural environment. Stop, look and listen to your surroundings.

What do you notice?

Spend time quietly contemplating what is around you on a daily basis without interference from external distractions.

How do you feel as a result?

- Alert?

- Focused?

- In-Tune?

- Clear?

Take a few moments to jot down some of your thoughts, reflections and any ideas which came to mind as you took a walk or sat back and allowed yourself to unwind.

## ◉ Launch Idea

---

### Create Five Year Goals

Write a letter to yourself from the future.

Five years from now who will you be, what will you be doing and did you achieve your leadership goals?

Seal the letter.

Read it in five years and see what's changed.

**NOW**

Send the letter to a trusted friend and ask for feedback.

# △ Self-Awareness Stimulator

## Rules

Work with a trusted colleague or friend to share three rules you would like to keep and three rules you'd like to change. Share your reasons for the change.

Three Rules I'd like to keep are:

1.

2.

3.

Three Rules I'd like to change are:

1.

2.

3.

STRATEGIZE:

- My strategy for change involves...

- I will begin to take action by...

Present your strategy to your colleague and ask for specific and actionable feedback:

- Is my strategy understandable and convincing?

- What made it powerful?

- What would you do differently if you were me?

△ Self-Awareness Stimulator

## Handling Change

No matter what age you are, life has a way of interrupting what you are doing and inserting a challenge into your life that was unexpected, unplanned and often-times, unwanted.

What do you do when this occurs?

Most of the time, individuals react and respond in the best possible way as the interruption is occurring. What can make a difference, however, is to examine those interruptions in retrospect and learn as much as possible from them.

When life interrupts again, you will have more experience and knowledge from which to gather inner strength, courage and determination to meet your challenges.

Reflect on an interruption that you had during the recent past.

What happened? Was there an event that precipitated the interruption or did it literally come at you suddenly and without warning?

*How did you respond?*

*Are you pleased with how you handled the situation?*

*Would you rather have reacted differently?*

*What could have made a difference?*

If that particular interruption happened again, how would you react in the present time?

Are there any resources or new knowledge that you need to acquire to be better prepared in the future?

What lesson did you learn from the interruption?

Perhaps you learned a valuable lesson and have now incorporated it into your life.

It's important to take time to reflect on these experiences. Think how, as a leader, you might incorporate the lesson in a story or example when you are helping others learn from similar experiences.

## This is the path of leadership

Leaders learn and they teach others based on their experience, wisdom and knowledge.

# △ Self-Awareness Stimulator

## Decision-Making

As the tension builds between the aspiring leaders' current challenges and present situations, new choices present themselves.

What do the choices you make under pressure say about you?

If you were the protagonist or hero in a movie, how do you react to pressure, stress, calamity, strife, injury, illness, misfortune, or accident?

As the hero in the story, people know, based on your reactions and behavior whether you have the integrity, honesty, truthfulness, courage, intelligence and cleverness to deal with situations.

The audience would also know the quality of your character, how authentic you are or have been until that moment when you were tested.

Life always presents challenges to carefully crafted plans and visions.

How you handle yourself in times of challenge or crisis will define you as a leader.

If you've been a fake or a flake, the world will see you for who you really are. If you have intentionally deceived others they will know you for the person that was hiding behind a mask, personal charisma, and a charming personality.

The bottom line?

**It's your choice!**

# △ Self-Awareness Stimulator

The following questions will assist you in uncovering the traits, qualities, talents, attributes, attitudes and concepts that will provide necessary new knowledge.

Given the work and self-reflection you have been doing so far, has anything changed?

1. What do I want from my life?

2. What is my personal vision?

3. What goals will support my vision?

4. What is the central, controlling idea for my life that I will hold myself accountable for achieving?

5. Who do I need to meet, talk with or read about who can provide me with a new perspective on the challenges I'll face as I forge a new leadership identity?

6. How did they become who they are now? What attitudes and behaviors do they exhibit? What are their habits, disciplines, and focuses of mind, body and spirit?

7. How can I best replicate what I admire most in others who have the qualities and skill-sets that I desire for myself?

8. Will they help me, mentor or coach me based on my desired achievements?

9. How open am I to feedback and constructive criticism from others whom I respect and admire?

10. How do I incorporate that new knowledge or information into my own repertoire toward changing some habit or behavior that is undesirable or that I could improve?

11. What matters most to me?

12. What are some of the things that I want to see change in my world?

13. Who do I need to be – my leadership identity – so that I can make a difference in those areas?

14. Who can help me think through the opportunities and challenges?

## ▶ Framework

IT IS IMPORTANT TO REMEMBER LEARNING IS AN ITERATIVE PROCESS AND NOT A LINEAR PROGRESSION.

WHAT YOU HOLD AS RIGHT AND TRUE ABOUT YOURSELF, OTHERS, ENVIRONMENT, WORK AND LIFE WILL EVOLVE AS YOU CONTINUE TO RELFECT AND CONSIDER THE PERSON YOU ARE NOW AND THE PERSON YOU COULD BE.

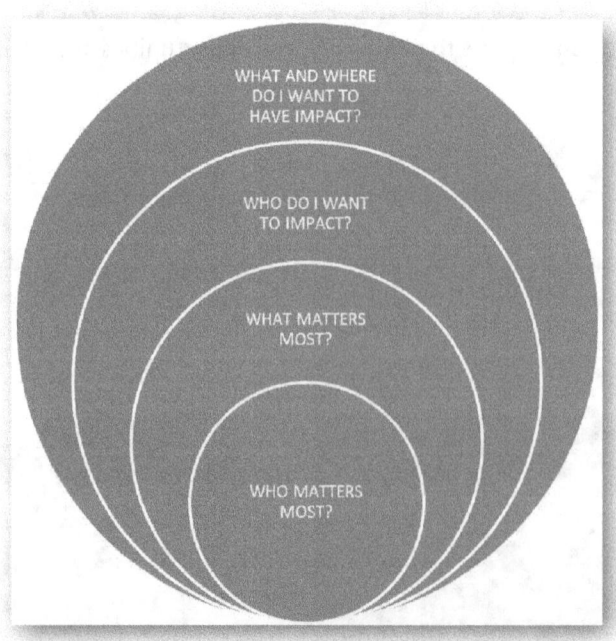

# △ Self-Awareness Stimulator

## Habits

Do your habits help or hinder you from achieving your goals?

Do they push you further away or do they enable you to get what you want?

List the habits you'd like to change and those that support your goals.

Plan for how you will go about changing them.

Create a list of short term and long term objectives.

# Ω  Pulse Check

CURRENT REALITY

- What are you doing?

- How are you feeling?

- What are you thinking?

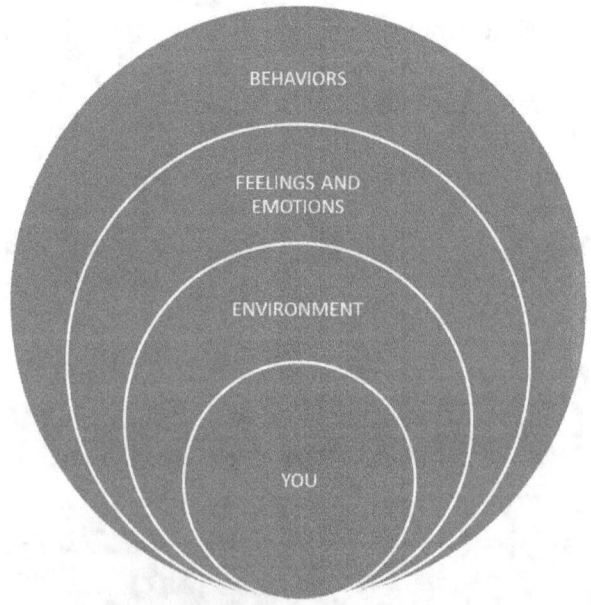

# △ Self-Awareness Stimulator

## Current Reality

**Remember. It will either open up more opportunities or create obstacles on the path to achieving your vision and goals.**

Now it is time to hit the pause button and take a few moments to reflect on your current situation or reality.

Questions can act as powerful triggers to help you explore what may be unexamined areas of your thinking process. Rather than shutting off the mind with repetitive mantras or entertainment, use questions to stimulate and empower yourself.

A leader is always focused on the present task at hand, while also looking and thinking ahead. Learning how to be strategic while implementing essential tactics is a key leadership ability and must be cultivated. It's important to know where you are strong and where you are weak in this area of competence.

**Begin with an examination of who you are, what you value and what's important to you.**

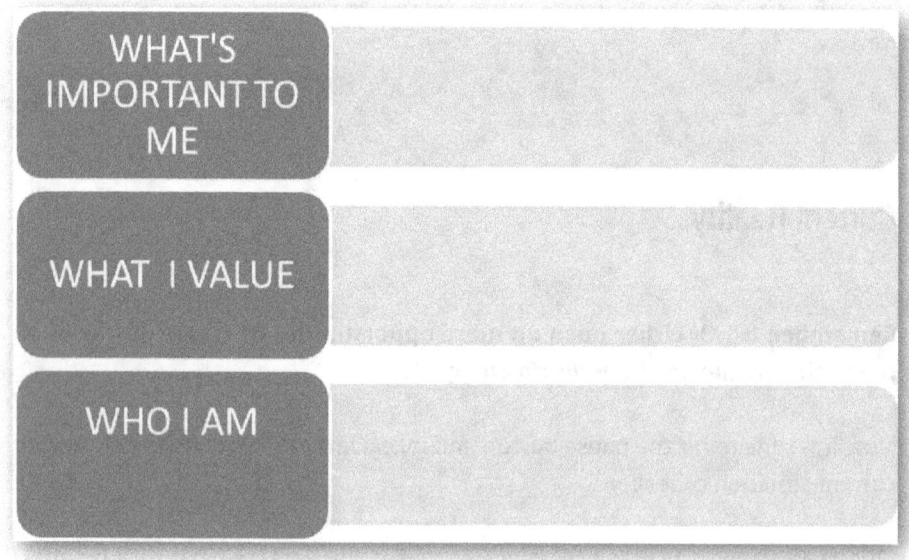

# △ Self-Awareness Stimulator

Use these questions to conduct a thorough self-examination. Based on the previous work, what new insights have been gained in these areas:

## Questions of Self-Reflection
- How did I come to be who I am today? Was it by chance or accident?
- Who would I be if no one were there to tell me what I could do or where I could go?
- What is the purpose of my life?
- Are my actions a result of what others have advised me to do or based on my own judgment?
- What am I doing that I am proud of?
- What am I sorry about or regret?
- What can people count on me for?

## Questions of Faith
- From where do I draw my strength?
- Where do I find solace and comfort in times of strife?
- When my patience and tolerance are tested, how do I react?
- What do I reach for when I am confused, angry, in despair, lonely, or anxious? People? Material objects? Inner guidance?

## Questions of Trust
- Do people seek my opinions?
- Do people turn to me in time of need?

- Do people ask me to lead activities, other people, and projects?
- Am I sought after as a person, a friend, or a neighbor?

## Questions of Caring for Self and Others

- Who in my life counts on me?
- What do I do to ensure that I am healthy - financially, emotionally, psychologically and physically?

## Questions of Responsibility

- Who do I blame when things go wrong?
- How do I handle disappointment and failure?
- Do I walk toward or away from risk - whether personal, financial or emotional?

## Feedback

Another tool with which you can successfully invite individuals to provide you with relevant and useful feedback is to ask colleagues or friends a few focused questions.

Ask for a brief meeting or request the feedback through an email.

As a colleague, client or business partner, what do you:

*Appreciate most about me?*

*Think might be limiting me?*

*Believe are my best qualities?*

*Think are my strengths, talents and qualities?*

The feedback you obtain in this manner can be very enlightening and provide you with valuable insights as to how your behavior is impacting those with whom you have daily and consistent contact.

Once again, thank the individuals for the time and energy. You might also offer to provide the same service to them if they think it would be helpful.

## SELF-REFLECT

Is asking for feedback becoming easier or more difficult?
Is the feedback making you more aware of your behavior?
Are the things you are learning about yourself motivating you?

## ◆ Fast Track Action

## **Feedback**

Oftentimes, people are reluctant to solicit feedback. However, with a moderate amount of structure and preparation it can be accomplished comfortably and with results. In PART I, you began the process of asking for feedback. Now you will take this activity to the next level.

You can begin by identifying several individuals who you trust will honor your request for feedback.

Write an explanatory email, asking the individuals for a few minutes of their time. A twenty-minute meeting, structured around a set of questions which you will provide, will be required.

What qualities do I have, that if I did more of them, would make me more effective?

What qualities do you most appreciate about me?

What is difficult about me? What part of me is difficult to get along with?

How might I be limiting myself or keeping myself back from accomplishing what I know I can achieve?

## SELF-REFLECT

Were you more comfortable asking for feedback this time around?
Did you allow yourself to be more vulnerable and open?
What was particularly uncomfortable for you?

## ◆ Fast Track Action

S end a letter of thanks to the individuals who took the time and energy to provide you with feedback.

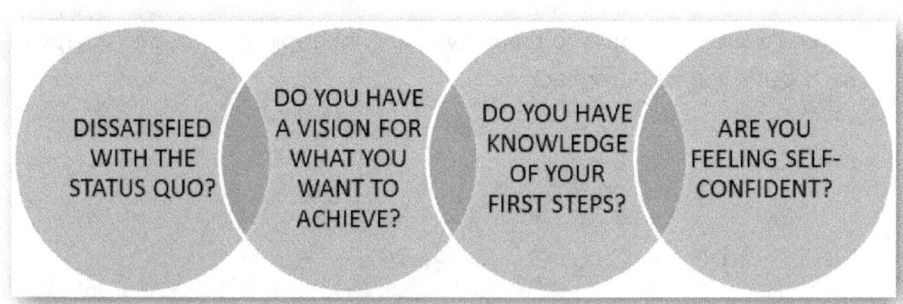

## Are You Ready For The Journey?

The following questions require only a "yes or no" answer:

1. Am I sufficiently dissatisfied with the way things are now that I am willing to invest the time and energy in creating a vision for leadership in life?

2. Will I be able to build up enough momentum so that I get past the wall of inertia, fear and intimidation I'll feel when I reach the point where I am paralyzed by the magnitude of what I am attempting to do?

3. Do I have the guts to take those first steps?

4. And if I can't, do I have the courage to ask for help?

## Who Am I? What Is My Identity?

There are numerous books and movies that present characters with well-defined values. Carefully choose what you read and watch. You will be influenced by what you experience.

## ◙ Launch Idea

---

## Be Your Own Best Self

It takes time, work, perseverance and courage, with enough fortitude to continue traveling the road to acquiring the competencies, traits, attitudes and abilities you will need for a future that you will create as a leader of your life.

Be an individual; be the leader of your own life. What you will win is your freedom that is independent of other thoughts, opinions or judgments of you.

How did you come to be who you are right now? These are two very important questions to consider whether or not you need to COURSE CORRECT at this point in the journey:

**What's working?**

**What's not working?**

**Do you like the results?**

Sometimes you need to recreate yourself in order to have a different future. Change does take time even when we wish it wouldn't.

If you continue doing what you are already doing, thinking and behaving you'll just get more of what you already have. Life itself will send along challenges, opportunities and obstacles your way.

Reacting to what life sends you is different from proactively creating what it is you want to happen even though life itself will continue to challenge you.

**Do you want to be in charge of the change or be at the effect of it?**

△ Self-Awareness Stimulator

## Developing High Levels of Self-Awareness

As in everything else that you do to create the life and work you desire, there are certain factors that will determine the difference between success and failure.

Learning how to develop your leadership abilities is no exception to the rule.

A critical factor in any kind of learning is AWARENESS.

Awareness is a critical building block determining the speed at which you will be able to achieve mastery at being a leader in life.

What does awareness mean?

Awareness is not an event or a transaction.

It is:

A state of being open to new information while weighing and choosing between conflicting streams of incoming data in order to determine next moves or actions.

It is not action itself or a substitute for action.

What is required?

- Attentiveness

- Intent

- Use the senses to engage the environment around you

Some may refer to "awareness" as "mindfulness".

Awareness requires you to be a fully conscious human being as in noticing things that are taking place both within yourself and in your surroundings or environment.

Awareness is about going beyond the day to day mindlessness and into a state of sensitivity to what is happening immediately and what could emerge as a result of circumstances or situations. This might also be referred to as 'critical thinking".

Leaders need to do this all the time. It takes work and energy. People who achieve success in life are super aware most of the time.

# △ Self-Awareness Stimulator

## What Influences You?

Nearly every waking moment of modern life is filled with messages. They come from the websites, apps, social media, family members, friends, work, teachers and the anecdotal bits and pieces of conversations heard in public places.

Where do you get the information you need to help you form your own opinions, judge situations and determine what you think, feel and know about something?

Who do you rely upon to help you sort through the complex and sometimes confusing mass of information and data that you are bombarded with every day?

You will not find the information and knowledge you need in text messages or sound bites from social media sources. You will need to sift through the mounds of information to find your truth.

This is a critical leadership task.

It is a discovery process and due diligence is required in order to separate what is real and what is not. In an age of information overload, this is not easy.

---

## Leadership Change Process

To achieve greater levels of effectiveness leaders are consistently in a state of learning.

Begin with where you are right now in life:

Assess your capacity and capabilities for leadership

Identify gaps based on self-imposed limitations and ingrained beliefs, cultural conditions, assumptions, judgments and attitudes.

Answering the above question, reflecting on the answers and considering different perspectives is a tall order. But that is where leadership begins.

In any goal achievement process, it is important to keep moving forward with the goal or goals in a clear line of sight.

Remaining vigilant to threats and open to opportunities is essential to increasing odds of achieving your intended results.

Keeping open to incoming information is vital. Self-awareness is key. Our environment is always giving us feedback. What is done with the feedback and how it's handled will determine the outcome of most endeavors.

# Leaders are Always Learning from their Experiences.

---

# Learning from Einstein's Definition of Insanity

*"Doing the same thing over and over again expecting a different result."*

Without a clear concept of your own history you will only be adding to more of what you already have. And that may not be nearly enough to get you to a place where you want and need to be in order to live a meaningful and purposeful life.

There may be something aching within you that wants to be expressed. You're not certain what it is and no one can tell you. You will need to discover this on your own.

Everything and everyone else is merely the "material" which can support you in your quest. Conversations, books and retreats will only get you so far.

It's important to remember that nothing stays exactly the same.

Either you are in charge of the change or you are at the effect of it.

Remaining in a position of "status quo" or stationary will only set you up to be a "sitting duck".

Regardless, no matter where you are or think you are right now, the path of leadership is a never-ending process of learning and growing.

**Leadership is active involvement and engagement with life.**

As already stated, getting there is not without its demands and costs in terms of time, energy and resources.

It may even cost you financially. You may choose a less lucrative path over one that could give you a greater monetary and ego-feeding payback.

Once again, only you can be the decider. No one else can do this important work of assessment but you.

# Leaders End with a Call to Action.

# Apply What You Learned with a Social Impact Initiative

**PROBLEM
TO BE
SOLVED**

**DISRUPTIVE
IDEA OR
INNOVATION**

**WHO BENEFITS?**

**SOCIAL & ECONOMIC
IMPACT RESULTS**

SPECIAL ACKNOWLEDGEMENT TO MY
MENTORS AND TEACHERS IN LIFE

My Father, Carmen Pagano

Dr. John Bell

Frank G. Hickey

Dr. Stephen John

Dr. Anne Lovett

Sister Helena Mary, I.H.M.

LuEsther Mertz

Joan Rose

www.ingramcontent.com/pod-product-compliance
Lightning Source LLC
Chambersburg PA
CBHW072301200526
45168CB00014B/121